AND
POWER

GRACE AND POWER

by

Reverend W. H. Griffith Thomas, D.D.

THOMAS NELSON PUBLISHERS
Nashville • Camden • New York

Copyright © 1984 Thomas Nelson Publishers

All rights reserved. Written permission must be secured from the publisher to use or reproduce any part of this book, except for brief quotations in critical reviews or articles.

Published in Nashville, Tennessee, by Thomas Nelson, Inc. and distributed in Canada by Lawson Falle, Ltd., Cambridge, Ontario.

Printed in the United States of America.

Unless otherwise noted, all Scripture references are from THE NEW KING JAMES VERSION. Copyright © 1979, 1980, 1982, Thomas Nelson, Inc., Publishers.

ISBN 0-8407-5934-7

To
*all the valued friends
at Keswick and elsewhere,
who have taught so many of us
how to "possess our possessions"*

Contents

Foreword 7
Preface 9

Part I: Provision for the Christian life

I Grace 13
II Justification 27
III Sanctification 39
IV Consecration 59

Part II: Protection for the Christian life

V Meditation...69
VI Prayer...79
VII Faithfulness 85
VIII Obedience 93

Part III: Possibility for the Christian life

IX Knowledge 107
X Power 123
XI Privilege...135
XII Satisfaction 149

O Lord, we beseech Thee mercifully to receive the prayers of Thy people which call upon Thee; and grant that they may both perceive and know what things they ought to do, and also may have grace and power faithfully to fulfill the same; through Jesus Christ our Lord. Amen.

—*Collect for the First Sunday after the Epiphany*

FOREWORD

An author whose works are still being published and reprinted more than half a century after his death is worth getting to know. I would like to introduce one such outstanding writer, Dr. W. H. Griffith Thomas (1861-1924).

Although I was not privileged to meet him, my father heard him speak at New York's then well-known "Tent Evangel" in the World War I era. My father was proud to have included Griffith Thomas among the many famous preachers from England and America that he heard in his youth. My next exposure to Griffith Thomas was when my oldest brother gave me two or three of his books as he left for the mission field and I was in Bible college. Later, while mounting a major exhibit of Griffith Thomas books and memorabilia at Dallas Theological Seminary's Mosher Library, I got to know the author's daughter, Winifred G. T. Gillespie, who has edited many of her father's books.

Though Griffith Thomas died many years before I was born, these three "encounters" in my personal experience illustrate, though in reverse order from his career, the three major phases of Dr. Griffith Thomas's ministry.

It was during the later part of his life especially that the author became known as a sought-after conference and church speaker among the English speaking community, especially the Keswick Movement.

The books on Genesis, Peter, and John that Dick bequeathed to me are just samples of the many outstanding works of Christian exposition from the pen of this fine writer. Clarity, simplicity, logically outlined presentation, and sheer readability characterize all of Griffith Thomas's work.

My alma mater, Dallas Theological Seminary, was cofounded by Griffith Thomas, and he would have been the first systematic theology professor when the school opened in 1924. This, however, was not to be, for he was removed in death the summer before the first semester started. He had served as principal of Wycliffe Hall, at his alma mater, Oxford, and later as lecturer at Wycliffe College, Toronto.

Grace and Power was originally published in 1916, nearly seventy years ago, yet is still fresh and relevant to the earnest Christian. I am happy that Thomas Nelson Publishers decided to reissue this fine little gem for late twentieth-century readers. As Executive Editor of the New King James Bible, I was most pleased with the decision to update the Bible text to this more readable version.

And now, let Dr. Griffith Thomas tell you in his own preface what is in store for you in *Grace and Power*.

Arthur L. Farstad

PREFACE

It is a fact, perhaps a significant fact, that throughout the Epistles of the New Testament, where, naturally, we find full instructions for Christians, there is only one exhortation to do the work of evangelization (2 Tim. 4:5), while appeals to carry out the duty of foreign missions are equally conspicuous by their absence. On the other hand, the Christian life, its provisions and possibilities, its secrets and methods, its duties and responsibilities, will be found emphasized almost everywhere.

Is there any connection between the silence and the emphasis? May it not be a reminder that when the Christian life is what it should be, the duty of evangelization at home and abroad will be the natural and necessary outcome, as effect to cause, as stream to source? Be this as it may, there can be no question about the way in which the New Testament calls attention to the Christian life and demands the highest possible standard while providing the fullest possible power.

The believer's life is described in the New Testament under two aspects: "acceptable to God and approved by men" (Rom. 14:18). We are to "walk and please God" (1 Thess. 4:1); to "walk worthy of the Lord unto all pleasing" (Col. 1:10); and to "do those things that are pleasing in His sight" (1 John 3:22). Nothing can be more inspiring than this requirement, leading us to pray, "Teach me to do the thing that pleases Thee" (Ps. 143:10; Prayer Book Version).

But the life of the Christian is also to be "approved by men." This is one of the best recommendations of the gospel the believer claims to possess, for nothing so readily impresses and attracts those around us as reality in daily living. When the Seven were appointed, one requirement was that they should be "men of honest report," that is, "well spoken of," men of good reputation. This feature is more prominent in the New Testament than many imagine (Acts 10:22; 16:2; 22:12; Eph. 5:15; Col. 4:5; 1 Thess. 4:12; 1 Tim. 3:7). It has been said that the "Christian is the world's Bible and sometimes they will read no other." All the more necessary, therefore, that we should be in "favor with God and man" (Luke 2:52) and thereby show that

> Our lips and lives express
> The Holy Gospel we profess.

This book is intended, in its first part, to call attention to some of the provisions of Christian living; in the second, to a few of its guarantees of protection; and in the third, to some of the possibilities of Christian living.

It embodies the substance of addresses given at various places in England and the United States.

W.H.G.T.

PART I

Provision for the Christian Life

"My grace is sufficient for you."—*2 Cor. 12:9*

"Having all sufficiency in all things."—*2 Cor. 9:8*

"Thoroughly equipped."—*2 Tim. 3:17*

"What He had promised, He was also able to perform."
—*Rom. 4:21*

I

GRACE

Our Lord came that there might be a gospel to preach. Then He sent His apostles to preach it. The gospel that He was in His person, that He provided by His Word, and the gospel that they received and proclaimed is best stated in the one word, *grace:* "The gospel of the grace of God"; "the grace of our Lord Jesus Christ"; "the Word of His grace."

What do we mean by *grace*? It is a large word, a great word, an all-inclusive word, perhaps the greatest word in the Bible, because it is the word most truly expressive of God's character and attitude in relation to man. It translates two or three roots in the Hebrew and Greek. In the Greek we find words and derivatives meaning "grace," "gift," to "give freely," to "forgive," to "bestow graciously," "joy," to "rejoice," "thanksgiving," to "give thanks" "thankful." In English (derived from the Latin) we have "grace," "gratis," "gratitude," "grateful," "gracious," "gratuity," "graceful," and such opposites as "ungrateful," "ungracious," "disgraceful." The subject is large and has many aspects; the passages, too, are numerous and well worthy of the closest study.

What does the word mean? The root seems to mean "to give pleasure," and then it branches out comprehensively in two directions: one in relation to the Giver; the other in relation to the receiver of the pleasure. Grace is first a quality of *graciousness* in the Giver and then a quality of *gratitude* in the recipient, which in turn makes him *gracious* to those around him.

But the idea has two distinct yet connected aspects even when applied only to God the Giver. It expresses the divine *attitude* to man as guilty and condemned. Grace refers to God's favor and good will toward us (Luke 1:30). So the mother of our Lord is described as permanently "favored" ("graced," Luke 1:28). This favor is manifested without any regard to merit; indeed, grace and merit are entire opposites. Grace is thus spontaneous (no promptings come from the outside), free (no conditions are required), generous (no restraint is shown), and abiding (no cessation is experienced). It is also (like favor) opposed to *wrath*, which means "judicial displeasure against sin." Further, it must be distinguished from mercy even though mercy is one of its methods of expression. Mercy is related to misery and (negatively) to the nondeserving. Grace is related to redemption and (positively) to the undeserving.

It then expresses the divine *action* to man as needy and helpless. Grace means not merely favor but also help; not only benevolence but also benefaction; not simply feeling but also force; not solely good will but also good work. It is divine favor expressed in and proved by His gift; attitude shown by action. Thus from *grace* comes *gift*, which invariably implies a gift of or by grace (Rom. 5:15; 1 Cor. 4:6; Rom. 12:6).

These two ideas are thus connected and united as cause and effect. They tell of God's heart and God's hand. Etymologically, therefore, *grace* is a term that refers to the beautiful, which gives delight. Theologically, it means

GRACE

God's favor as seen in His gift. Practically, it implies God's presence and redemptive power in human life. Blending all these aspects we may think of grace as God's *spontaneous gift* which causes *pleasure* and produces *blessing*. Hort defines grace as "free bounty" and, as such, it produces joy and is the cause of actual power in daily living. It includes the two ideas of God's attitude and God's action; His graciousness and His gift; His pleasure and His provision; His benediction and His benefaction. In a sentence, we may define God's grace as His favor to the sinner, that favor being shown and proved by His gift.

Paul is pre-eminently the apostle of grace. Out of one hundred fifty-five New Testament references to it, one hundred thirty are his, directly or indirectly. Grace opens and closes his epistles. Grace is the keynote of his teaching. Grace was the secret of his life from conversion to close. By the grace of God, he was what he was, suffered what he suffered, and accomplished what he accomplished. More, perhaps, than any other man, he found grace to be the primary characteristic of his Christianity.

Grace is the predominant feature of the Bible. There is no grace in heathen religions. It is not a pre-Christian word or idea. Ugliness not grace, cruelty not grace, merit not grace mark other religions.

It is therefore worthwhile to ponder this wonderful truth, and to look at it in the varied light provided by Holy Scripture.

What Is Grace in God?

Grace is God's mercy pitying. We can never speak of grace without speaking of sin. It was sin that prompted

GRACE AND POWER

grace. At first God "saw" that everything was very good (Gen. 1). Then alas! He "saw" that every imagination of man's heart was only evil continually (Gen. 6). And then He "saw" that there was "no man, and wondered that there was no intercessor" (Is. 59:16). This threefold "sight" led to the revelation and provision of grace, for "His own arm brought salvation."

Grace is God's wisdom planning. To see was to ponder and plan, and the promise of Eden (Gen. 3:16) runs through the entire Old Testament. Indeed, we may go farther back and think of the divine purpose of grace "before the world began." As we study what is said both of what God has done "*from* the foundation of the world" ("from," Rev. 13:8) and of what He purposed *before* it ("before," Eph. 1:4), we can see a little of the plan of grace in the eternal wisdom of God.

Grace is God's power preparing. For four thousand years the grace of God was at work, and the divine preparation went on. Among the Jews a Savior was prepared for the world, and among the Gentiles the world was prepared for a Savior. Dimly realized by patriarchs, the truth became gradually clearer through the ages by means of Moses and the prophets, until the end of the old dispensation. At length in the fullness of time the preparations were complete, and Christ came. The primeval invitation had been given when first God "bade many," and then when the preparations were made, the second invitation was given: "Come, for all things are now ready" (Luke 14:17).

Grace is God's love providing. The pity, the plan, and the preparation were all prompted by love, for "God so loved the world that He gave His only begotten Son" (John 3:16), and when Christ appeared He was the revelation of the "grace of God that brings salvation" (Titus 2:11). We note that it was bringing, not sending, for His character was "full of grace and truth."

God is rightly revealed as "the God of all grace," and Christianity as the religion of grace. In nature we see pre-eminently the wisdom, the majesty, and the power of God. In providence we see the law, the righteousness, and the justice of God. In heathenism we see ugliness, hardness, and cruelty. But in Christianity we see grace, because it issues from the very heart of God Himself. The word *grace* expresses more definitely than any other term the principle on which God deals with men. It is the very opposite of all human ideas and principles. Human life knows of justice, and accordingly of dealing out rewards and punishments. Man is aware of the meaning of law and its results on innocent and guilty. Man is familiar with culture, education, progress, and discipline as processes in life. But by nature he knows nothing of grace. The idea of dealing with sinfulness and unworthiness as God has done in the gospel by grace and of making its iniquity the occasion for superabundant blessing is so utterly unlike all things human, that we can only speak of it in the words of God through the prophet: "My thoughts are not your thoughts, nor are your ways My ways, says the LORD. For as the heavens are higher than the earth, so are My ways higher than your ways, and My thoughts than your thoughts" (Is. 55:8–9).

Grace means more, far more than we can put into words, because it means nothing less than the infinite character of God Himself. It includes mercy for the undeserving and unmerciful, help for the helpless and hopeless, redemption for the renegade and repulsive, love for the unloving and unlovely, kindness for the unkind and unthankful. And all this in full measure and overflowing abundance, because of nothing in the object, and because of everything in the giver, God Himself.

Grace is the character of God, including mercy and truth, righteousness and peace. Grace is the union of love and holiness, the very foundation of the nature of God in Christ.

What Is Grace in Christ?

It is saving grace. This is suggested by the name *Jesus*, which means "salvation" (Matt. 1:21), and the Apostle rejoiced to say, and said it twice, "By grace you have been saved." The full statement calls for attention. "God, who is rich in mercy, because of His great love with which He loved us, even when we were dead in trespasses, made us alive together with Christ (by grace you have been saved), and raised us up together in the heavenly places in Christ Jesus, that in the ages to come He might show the exceeding riches of His grace in His kindness toward us in Christ Jesus" (Eph. 2:4–7). Divine inspiration seems to have endeavored to exhaust itself in the effort to express the glory of grace. Not only mercy but "rich in mercy." Not only love but "His great love with which He loved us." Not only grace but "the exceeding riches of His grace." And to make it still more beautifully human, the culminating point is "His kindness toward us in Christ Jesus." And then this is seen to be the source of our salvation. "For by grace you have been saved through faith, and that not of yourselves; it is the gift of God" (Eph. 2:8). It is grace, as we have seen, that purposed salvation, grace that purchased it, grace that proclaimed

GRACE

it, and it is grace that applies it to our souls. We did not deserve it, we could not provide it, we do not primarily seek it. From first to last, salvation is all of grace.

> O the love that sought me,
> O the blood that bought me,
> O the grace that brought me to the fold.

Whether, therefore, we think of the condemnation or of the guilt of sin, the only way of deliverance is "by grace." Grace is the gift purchased for us by the tribunal that found us guilty. No merit, no effort, no payment of man can effect salvation. "Not of works, lest anyone should boast" (Eph. 2:9). There are only two classes of men in this world: those who think they can win or earn God's favor; the others who are certain they cannot. The former approach God and say,

> *Something* in my hand I bring.

The latter say,

> *Nothing* in my hand I bring,
> Simply to Thy cross I cling.

The hand clings to the cross, and this alone *fills* it with "something." The reason why trust is so emphasized is that it expresses at once the cessation of dependence on self and the commencement of dependence on someone else. And this explains how Paul can ring out the gospel, "By grace you have been saved, through faith." It is not because of our tears of repentance or prayers that He saves us; it is not even because of the strength of the faith by which we accept Him that He accepts us; it is not because of any pledge of future faithfulness that He receives us; it is not because of His foresight of our subsequent obedience that He is willing to take us back. It is solely of His unmerited mercy, His undeserved grace, and His unrequited love that He welcomes us to Himself.

> That Thou should'st love a wretch like me,
>   And be the God Thou art,
> Is darkness to my intellect,
>   But sunshine to my heart.

It is sanctifying grace. This is suggested by the word *Christ*, which means "anointed." Jesus Christ the Savior was anointed by the Holy Spirit, and this anointing was given to Him for His people (Acts 2:33). He is "Christ," the Anointed One, and they are "Christians," the anointed ones (Acts 11:26). This anointing of Christ by the Spirit is for holiness. Grace not only brings salvation but sanctification. A very usual conception of the Christian life is that of salvation by grace, but sanctification by our own effort; justification by faith, but sanctification by fighting; salvation by acceptance, but sanctification by struggle. But God does not rescue and redeem us from the horrible pit and miry clay, set our feet upon a rock, and then expect us to go on alone. This way would lead to disappointment and often backsliding. No, "He orders our goings." The grace that saves is the grace that sanctifies. "As you have therefore received Christ Jesus the Lord, so walk in Him" (Col. 2:6). We received Him by grace through faith; we must continue by the same way and walk the same step. There is grace "wherein we stand" as well as grace whereby we have been saved, and this grace

GRACE

sanctifies, fills, and keeps. Goodness is not a matter of temperament with grace merely supplementing nature. Goodness is not culture and education, as though grace means only the introduction of high ideals, powerful motives, and splendid models by which to face the old sinful nature. The seventh chapter of Romans with its deadly warfare of two natures does not represent the normal Christian life of sanctification. There is no divine grace in that chapter; only man's nature struggling to be good and holy by law. The processes of penance and self-mortification are only examples of this endeavor to be holy by effort, struggle, and law. God's way is all of grace, the gift of Christ by the Holy Spirit entering in to abide, to cleanse, to keep, to guide, to overcome, to transform. Grace does not improve the old nature; it overcomes it. Grace does not educate the natural heart; it promises hereafter to uproot it. Meanwhile grace counteracts the tendencies of the natural heart and enables the believer to "reign in life." Grace means a new life, a divine life, which lifts us above the natural and is nothing else than the life of Christ Himself in His people. This is what John meant when he said, "Of His fullness we have all received, and grace for grace" (John 1:16). Grace provides and produces what we require for holiness. Everything that we need—love, patience, holiness, meekness, in a word, Christlikeness—becomes ours as grace controls, and because it is not I, but Christ living in me.

Let no one say that grace is insufficient for holiness or that it excuses sin. Far from it, and quite the contrary. It teaches us to deny worldly lusts and to live soberly, righteously, and godly in this present world, and then it gives the power to do all this. The gospel is for life here and now, not merely for death. It provides not a hearse

GRACE AND POWER

but a chariot. It is intended to give a good soul, a sound mind, a healthy body, a strong nerve. It does not subtract from anything right or bright; it can "add" (2 Pet. 1:5), it is "multiplied" (2 Pet. 1:2), and it provides "abundance of grace" (Rom. 5:17). So far from dispensing with morality, it insists on it as essential, and not only so, but grace and grace alone secures morality in quality and quantity.

> Talk we of morals! O Thou bleeding Lamb,
> The best morality is love of Thee.

It is sovereign grace. This is suggested by the word *Lord*, which implies the rule and mastership of Christ Jesus. Paul tells us that grace "will reign" (Rom. 5:17), and this is so through "Jesus Christ our Lord" (Rom. 5:21). From the very outset to the very end He is and must be Lord.

"To this end Christ died and rose and lived again, that He might be Lord" (Rom. 14:9). And as this is realized His grace is seen to be sovereign, and the soul is called on to be humble. There is nothing so humbling as grace because we know it can only be ours in proportion as Jesus Christ is our Lord. "What do you have that you did not receive?" (1 Cor. 4:7). This is the constant and grateful language of the soul. "By the grace of God I am what I am" (1 Cor. 15:10).

It is satisfying grace. This is suggested by the full title, "Jesus Christ our Lord." Grace satisfies at every step. It meets the claim of law with justification; it meets the breach of love with forgiveness; it meets the consciousness of solitariness by fellowship; it meets the sense of misery by love; it meets the hideousness of defilement by holiness; it meets the realization of weakness by power; it meets the haunting of fear by hope. We can therefore look back and praise the grace that made us Christ's; we can look around and trust the grace that keeps us His; and we can look forward and hope fully for the grace that is to be brought to us in the revelation of Jesus Christ (1 Pet. 1:13).

> Grace fathomless as the sea,
> Grace flowing from Calvary.
> Grace enough for eternity,
> Grace for you and for me.

What Is Grace in Us?

Our life is to be a monument of grace. All that we are, have, do, and become is of grace, and we are to live so that our lives are to be to the "glory of His grace."

Our lips are to be mouthpieces of grace. We are to "testify to the gospel of the grace of God" (Acts 20:24). Our speech is to "be with grace" (Col. 4:6), and we are to sing "with grace in [our] hearts to the Lord" (Col. 3:16).

Our love is to be a means of grace. God's love is only made available for others through His children, and for this reason believers are to be "means of grace." The truth needed for salvation, the comfort needed for cheer, the holiness needed for living are mediated by us to others, and in proportion as they see the love of God in us will our lives be means of grace to them. Grace will make us gracious in our dealings and enable us to avoid the spirit of hardness, hatred, and severity and to manifest the spirit of love, patience, mildness, forgiveness, and tenderness. The love of God in our hearts will lead to the love of others, and all our relationships will be sweetened, hallowed, purified, uplifted, and transfigured. All this will be so powerful in its influence that those around will see God in us and will find our lives true means of desiring to come into contact with Him. There is no means of grace to compare with a Christlike spirit.

Our labor is to be a messenger of grace. The works of grace are to be carried out by God's people, and if they do not do this, they will thereby prove that they know nothing of grace. What we receive from God as *gratia* comes to us *gratis* and is intended to make us *gratum*, "grateful." His grace is intended to elicit gratitude, and gratitude is to be shown in graciousness to others. Yet all along it will be "Not I, but the grace of God which was with me" (1 Cor. 15:10). The Holy Spirit endows us with gifts of grace, and we minister according to the ability that God gives. Our sufficiency is not of self but of grace, and our service is the outflow of the grace of God in the heart. From Him we receive the love, the power, the blessing we endeavor to pass on to others; from Him comes the grace that enables us to serve God acceptably. Thus we indeed testify to the grace of God and reveal something of the exceeding riches of His grace.

As we review the marvelous record of grace in God, in Christ, and in us, we see very plainly two things. First, it is a gospel for the sinner. It excludes all human merit, renounces all human claim, and centers in God alone. If anyone should say, "It is too cheap," let him look at Calvary and see the cost to God. If anyone should say, "It is too easy," let him again look at Calvary and realize what was needed to put sin away. It is as if God were saying, "If you want to know what sin is, look at My Son." It *is* cheap, it *is* easy for us because it is gratuitous. If it were not gratuitous, there would be no salvation at all. But to God it was unspeakably costly, because sin was so hideous and awful as to necessitate it. But the "precious"

GRACE

blood of Christ is the glory of grace, and now to us who believe He is indeed "precious" and will be to all eternity.

Second, it is a gospel for the saint. It not only provides redemption but also humbles pride, guarantees holiness, inspires to service, incites to hope, pledges heaven, and glorifies God. No wonder, therefore, that we are invited to receive this grace and warned against receiving it in vain (2 Cor. 6:1). It calls for appropriation and application. Grace does not work apart from our responsibility. We must use it, believe it, respond to it, reproduce it. We can have little or much, we can be rich or poor, we can rejoice in the divine wealth or exist in miserable poverty. But those who accept the divine invitation know by experience what Paul meant when he said, "Those who receive abundance of grace and of the gift of righteousness will reign in life through the One, Jesus Christ" (Rom. 5:17).

And so, "the Lord will give grace and glory" (Ps. 84:11). First grace, then glory. No grace, no glory. Much grace, much glory. If grace, then glory. Be it ours to say *Amen*.

"Amen" as a prayer. May it be so!
"Amen" as a purpose. It shall be so!
"Amen" as a prospect. It will be so!
"Amen" as a persuasion. It can be so!
"Amen" as a possession. It is so!

> Grace! 'tis a charming sound,
>   Harmonious to the ear;
> Heav'n with the echo shall resound
>   And all the earth shall hear.
>
> Grace first contrived a way
>   To save rebellious man;

GRACE AND POWER

And all the steps that grace display,
   Which drew the wondrous plan.

'Twas grace that wrote my name
   In life's eternal book;
'Twas grace that gave me to the Lamb
   Who all my sorrows took.

Grace taught my wandering feet
   To tread the heav'nly road;
And new supplies each hour I meet
   While pressing on to God.

Grace taught my soul to pray,
   And made my eyes o'erflow;
'Twas grace which kept me to this day
   And will not let me go.

Grace all the work shall crown
   Through everlasting days;
It lays in heav'n the topmost stone,
   And well deserves the praise.

Oh, let Thy grace inspire
   My soul with strength divine!
May all my powers to Thee aspire,
   And all my days be Thine.

II
JUSTIFICATION

The spiritual life can be considered from the divine or the human standpoint, from the point of view of God's provision, or from that of our appropriation. As a rule differences do not show themselves in connection with the great objectives concerning God, Christ, the Holy Spirit, sin, and redemption. It is only in the application of them to individual and corporate life that differences emerge. We see this in the great Reformation movement of the sixteenth century. There were few essential differences on fundamental doctrine among the reformers; the vital differences were in regard to the precise methods of applying Christ's redemption to individual life. This is especially seen in connection with what is known as the doctrine of justification, for it was the theological and spiritual foundation of the Reformation movement. People sometimes wonder why Luther called that doctrine "the article of a standing or falling Church," but his spiritual insight was perhaps never more evident than when he did so.

The question of justification was not only the foundation of the Reformation; it lies at the root of all Christian life and service, for only when it is settled are real peace, power, and progress possible. The prominence given to it at the Reformation is a striking testimony to its importance as, in some respects, the supreme question of the ages. Justification is concerned with the great inquiry: "How can man be just with God?" This inquiry is found as far back as the book of Job, and then no less than four times (4:17; 9:2; 15:14; 25:4). It is seen throughout the history of the Jews; it is expressed in heathen sacrifices and is implied, in one way or another, in all oriental religions. The Bible alone gives the true answer, and it was this beyond all else that led to the emphasis on the Bible as the rule of faith at the time of the Reformation. It may be said that the whole movement of the sixteenth century was bound up with the two principles of the sufficiency and the supremacy of the Bible and justification by faith.

The first hint of the latter subject comes in Genesis 15:6, and then gradually through the Old Testament more and more light is given in such passages as Psalm 143:2, Micah 6:6, Habakkuk 2:4, until at length in the New Testament we have God's full revelation in answer to man's inquiry. It will help us to understand this subject if we proceed to ask some questions.

What Is the Meaning of Justification?

Justification can be understood either as the divine act and gift to man, or else as the human reception and result of the divine gift.

Justification is thus connected with our true relation to God. A good definition of it is found in the Church of England Article, "We are accounted righteous before God." Justification is not concerned with our spiritual

JUSTIFICATION

condition, but with our spiritual relation; not with our actual state, but with our judicial position. This should be continually borne in mind in order to avoid spiritual confusion and difficulty.

This true relation to God was originally lost by sin. Sin is always disobedience of the divine law, rebellion against God's will. In regard to our true relation to God, there are three results of sin: guilt, condemnation, and separation. We see these three in the Garden of Eden as the direct and immediate result of sin.

Justification is the restoration of this true relation to God, and as such includes (*a*) the removal of condemnation by the gift of forgiveness; (*b*) the removal of guilt by the reckoning (or imputation) of righteousness; and (*c*) the removal of separation by the restoration to fellowship. Justification therefore means "to treat as just or righteous," "to account righteous," "to regard as righteous," "to declare righteous," "to pronounce righteous in the eyes of the law" (Ps. 51:4; Prov. 17:15; Ezek. 16:51–52; Matt. 11:19; 12:37; Luke 7:35). As we have seen, it is at least a coincidence that Paul's three questions at the close of his eighth chapter in Romans deal with these three results of sin as seen in the history of the Fall: (*a*) "Who shall bring a charge against God's elect?" (verse 33). That is, no guilt. (*b*) "Who is he who condemns?" (verse 34). No condemnation. (*c*) "Who shall separate us?" (verse 35). No separation.

Justification is therefore much more than pardon, and the two are clearly distinguished by Paul (Acts 13:38–39). A criminal is pardoned, though he cannot be regarded as righteous. But justification is that act of God whereby He accepts and accounts us righteous, while in ourselves we are unrighteous. The Christian is not merely a pardoned criminal, but a righteous man. Man can forgive his fellow man, but he cannot justify him. God can do both. Forgiveness is an act issuing in an attitude. Forgiveness is repeated throughout life; justification is complete and never repeated. It relates to our spiritual position in the sight of God and covers the whole of our life—past, present, and future. Forgiveness is only negative, the removal of condemnation; justification is also positive, the removal of guilt and the bestowal of a perfect standing before God. In a word, justification means reinstatement. Forgiveness is being stripped; justification is being clothed. Day by day we approach God for forgiveness and grace, on the footing of a relation of justification that lasts throughout our lives. In regard to the justified man, the believer, God is "faithful and just to forgive" (1 John 1:9). Thus justification is the ground of our assurance. The reason why "we know" is because of what Christ has done for us and is to us.

Justification is also different from "making righteous," which is the usual interpretation of sanctification. The two are inseparable in fact, but they are distinguishable in thought and must certainly be kept quite clear of each other if we desire peace and blessing. Justification concerns our standing; sanctification, our state. The former affects our position; the latter, our condition. The first deals with relationship; the second, with fellowship. And even though they are bestowed together, we must never confuse them. The one is the foundation of peace—"Christ for us"; the other is the foundation of purity—"Christ in us." The one deals with acceptance; the other, with attainment. Sanctification admits of degrees, we may be more or less sanctified; justification has no degrees, but is

JUSTIFICATION

complete, perfect, and eternal. We are "justified from all things" (Acts 13:39). Our Lord indicated this distinction between justification and sanctification when He said, "He who is bathed [justification] needs only to wash his feet [sanctification]" (John 13:10).

At this point it is necessary and important to consider the Roman Catholic doctrine of justification. While there are other prominent differences between the New Testament and the church of Rome, it is apt to be overlooked that there is a fundamental difference between them on justification as well. A brief reference to what happened at the Council of Trent will enable us to understand this difference. One scholar described the statement put forth at that council as "a masterpiece of theological dexterity." This was doubtless due to the fact that not a little evangelical doctrine of the Roman church had to be considered, and so much was this the case, that at one time it had been thought possible to win over the Protestants. But that time, if it ever existed, had gone by, and the discussion in the council revealed fundamental lines of difference. A small minority was ready to accept the Lutheran view of justification by faith alone, but the majority easily won the day on behalf of a view that was almost the exact opposite of the Lutheran doctrine. The result was that justification was no longer regarded as a change of state, but as the actual conversion of a sinner into a righteous man. The fact is that Rome teaches forgiveness through sanctification, while Scripture teaches the opposite. Rome confuses justification and sanctification, and says that the former comes by the infusion of grace and includes remission and renovation. But this is really to rob the soul of the objective ground of righteousness and to confuse spiritual acceptance with spiritual attainment.

Justification in Scripture is independent of, and anterior to, the spiritual state or condition, which, however, necessarily follows. It has often been pointed out that justification, according to the Scripture, is complete from the first. As a modern writer has remarked, the father in the parable does not leave his prodigal son outside the house until he has shown his repentance by his works. He goes forth to meet him and heartily welcomes him. In the same way the sinner is not taken back into the divine favor by degrees but is restored at once to all his privileges as a child of God. This, as it has been well urged, is the only way to make the work of sanctification complete. It is a work that can go forward only after the relation of fatherhood and sonship has been fully reestablished. It is only by such love that the sinner's love can be made perfect (1 John 4:19).

It is of vital importance, therefore, to keep clear the distinction between the doctrine of the New Testament and that of Rome, because there is much confusion today in regard to the essential meaning of our acceptance with God.

What Is the Basis of Justification?

We are accounted righteous before God, "only on account of the merit of our Lord Jesus Christ." This is the language of the Anglican Article, and it can be parallelled by identical teaching in the Westminster Confession and other similar documents. It is an echo of the Pauline language, "By Him...justified" (Acts 13:39). The "merit" of our Lord Jesus Christ, of course, refers to His atoning work, by which He removed the alienation between God

JUSTIFICATION

and the sinner and brought about our reconciliation. We must never forget that the New Testament doctrine of reconciliation implies a change of relationship and not a mere alteration of feeling on our part. This doctrine of justification because of the work of Christ is seen all through the New Testament. Our Lord's perfect obedience, even unto death, His payment of the penalty due to our transgressions, His spotless righteousness, the entire merit of His divine person and work, form the ground or basis of our justification. This merit is reckoned to us, put to our account; God looks at us in Him not only as pardoned but also as righteous. "He made Him who knew no sin to be sin for us, that we might become the righteousness of God in Him" (2 Cor. 5:21). This is the great and satisfying doctrine of the imputed righteousness of Christ, which is clearly taught in the New Testament as meritorious on our behalf. It is sometimes stated that this theory is not found in Scripture, because of its association with what is sometimes called "legal fiction," but in the light of the teaching of the New Testament on our Lord's atoning death, by which we are accounted righteous before God, the doctrine of imputation is quite clear, and is taught plainly, in Scripture and therefore in the truest theology.

This reference to the "merit" of our Lord brings into greater contrast the negative aspect emphasized by Paul that our justification is due to Christ through faith and not from our own works or deservings. Our obedience to law could not merit or work out our justification. It is absolutely impossible for anything human to form the foundation of acceptance with God, for our obedience to law could not bring this about. God requires perfect obedience (Gal. 3:10), and man cannot render this. Human nature has ever been attempting to establish its own righteousness, but failure has been the invariable result. The Jews of old (Rom. 10:3) and mankind today alike fail because of the twofold inability: inability to blot out the past, and inability to guarantee the present and future. Justifying righteousness must be by a perfect obedience, and the Lord Jesus is the only One who ever rendered it. Nothing could be clearer in the New Testament than the absolute impossibility of human merit in connection with justification.

What Is the Method of Justification?

The merit of our Lord becomes ours "by faith." "By Him everyone who believes is justified" (Acts 13:39). Faith is never the ground of justification; it is only its means or channel. All the New Testament references to faith indicate this in the clearest possible way. Trust implies dependence upon another and the consequent cessation of dependence upon ourselves. Faith is therefore the acknowledgment of our own inability and the admission of our need of another's ability. Faith links us to Christ and is the means of our appropriation of His merit. The full meaning of faith in the New Testament is trust. (1) The primary idea is belief in a fact (1 John 5:1). (2) The next is belief in a person's work (John 4:21). (3) But the fullest is trust in a person (John 3:16). Thus, faith in its complete sense includes the assent of the mind and the consent of the will, the credence of the intellect and the confidence of the heart. As such, it is best understood as trust, the attitude of one person to another.

The reason faith is emphasized is that it is the only

JUSTIFICATION

possible answer to God's revelation. From the earliest days this has been so. The word of the Lord came to Abraham and he at once responded by simple trust (Gen. 15:1–6). To the same effect are the various illustrations of faith in Hebrews 11, all implying response to a previous revelation. Between man and man the absence of faith is a barrier to communion, and it is just the same in things spiritual. Faith in man answers to grace in God. Faith is the correlative of promise. Trust answers to truth; faith renounces self and emphasizes God's free gift. There is no merit in faith. It is self-assertion with a view to self-surrender. As one once said, "God doth justify the believing man, yet not for the worthiness of his belief, but for His worthiness who is believed." We are not justified by belief in Christ but by Christ in whom we believe. Faith is nothing apart from its object and is only valuable as it leads us to Him who has wrought a perfect righteousness, and as it enables us to appropriate Him as the Lord of our righteousness.

What Is the Value of Justification?

The Anglican Article speaks of the doctrine as "most wholesome" and "very full of comfort," which is not surprising because every revival of spiritual life has been associated with it as the true explanation of the way in which the Atonement is appropriated by sinful men.

Justification in Christ through faith is a necessity for spiritual health. The Council of Trent clearly taught the meritoriousness of good works. But as long as this is emphasized there cannot possibly be that spiritual life which is found in the New Testament. Justification by faith is the foundation of peace. The soul looks backward, outward, upward, onward, even inward, and is able to say with the Apostle, "justified from all things," and as a result of being "justified by faith, we have peace with God" (Rom. 5:1). When this is realized, all questions of human merit disappear, and the fabric of Roman Catholicism falls to the ground. This justification is immediate, certain, complete, and abiding.

Justification by faith is really the only answer to the moral perplexities of the doctrine of original sin. It vindicates God's righteousness while manifesting His mercy (Acts 17:30, RSV; Rom. 3:25, RSV). Our deepest need is a right idea of the character of the God with whom we have to do. How He can be just and yet justify the ungodly is an insoluble problem apart from Jesus Christ. Christ is the proof of God's capacity to forgive while remaining just. A sin-convicted soul demands at least as much righteous indignation of sin in God as it feels itself. This is seen in the Cross. It is characteristic of the apostle Paul's teaching in Romans that the Cross is the manifestation of God's righteousness rather than of His mercy (Rom. 3:21–26). In all this it will never be forgotten that faith is not the ground but only the means of our justification, and the strength or weakness of our trust will not affect the fact but only the enjoyment of our justification.

This doctrine is also the secret of spiritual liberty. All the Reformers felt and declared this, and we repeat it was with true spiritual insight that Luther spoke of it as "the article of a standing or falling Church"; indeed, we may go further and say with a modern writer that it is "the article of a standing or falling soul." It removes the bondage of the soul, sets the prisoner free, introduces him directly to

JUSTIFICATION

God, and gives continual access into the Holiest. It therefore cuts at the root of all sacerdotal mediation as both unnecessary and dangerous. On this account it is easy to understand the intense opposition shown to this doctrine on the part of the theologians of the church of Rome.

This doctrine is also the necessity for spiritual power. It is the foundation of holiness. The soul is introduced into the presence of God, receives the Holy Spirit, realizes the indwelling presence of Christ, and in these finds the secret and guarantee of purity of heart and life. It brings the soul into relation with God, so that from imputed righteousness comes imparted righteousness, and this keeps the doctrine from the charge of mere intellectual orthodoxy without spiritual vitality. Far from the doctrine's putting a premium upon carelessness, it is in reality one of the springs of holiness. When Paul was charged with what is now called antinomianism, or opposition to the law of God, he did not tone down his doctrine in the least but declared it all the more fully as the very heart of the gospel.

It is also the secret of true spiritual service. The soul released from anxiety about itself is free to show concern about others. The heart is at leisure from itself to set forward the salvation of those around. When Christian workers obtain a clear insight into this doctrine and yield their lives to its power and influence, it becomes the means of liberty to spiritual captives and the secret of peace and blessing to hearts in spiritual darkness and fear.

From all this it is easy to see what the New Testament teaches, the intense and immense spiritual blessing of the doctrine, and there are signs that the truth is being realized afresh by many who have been "tied and bound by the chain" of a purely legal view of Christianity. Certainly, if we are to get back not merely to the joy, peace, liberty, and power of Reformation days, but still more to the primitive truth of the Christian life recorded in the New Testament, we must give the most definite prominence to this truth of justification in Christ through faith.

III

SANCTIFICATION

If an average congregation, or even a Bible class, were asked, "Why did Jesus Christ die?" the answer in almost every case would probably be, "He died for our sins, in our stead." This would be all true but not all the truth. The purpose of the death of Christ is brought before us in the New Testament in a variety of ways, and each of them calls for careful attention. For our present purpose we must look at three passages: 2 Corinthians 5:15; Ephesians 5:25; Titus 2:14. When we do so we shall easily see that "for our sins" means salvation from at least three things: the penalty, the power, and the presence of sin. *Salvation* is one of the greatest and widest words in the New Testament, and it concerns the past, present, and future. It embraces justification, sanctification, and glorification. These three great truths are expressed for us in three phrases: *in* Christ, *like* Christ, *with* Christ, and at least one passage has all three in it (Acts 26:18).

We have already considered the first, justification; now we have to look at the second, which has an intimate and necessary connection with what has preceded. Justification is to sanctification as the foundation is to the building, the source to the stream, the cause to the effect. Let us, therefore, give heed to the teaching of 1 Thessalonians 4:3: "This is the will of God, your sanctification."

The Principle of Sanctification

Sanctification is a familiar word, but perhaps its very familiarity prevents us from understanding the two great truths involved and included in it.

Sanctification means, first of all, "consecration," or a true relation to God. It needs to be reiterated that the root idea of the Hebrew and Greek word for "holy," "sanctified," and their cognates is *separation*. The original idea seems to be ceremonial, and etymologically, that which is "holy" or "sanctified" means "that which belongs to God," the primary idea being not moral but ceremonial. This original meaning is seen in connection with days, places, institutions (as well as persons) being holy or sanctified, where the meaning can only be separation (Gen. 2:3; Ex. 13:2; Josh. 7:13). Thus sanctification, in its etymological sense, means "being set apart from other things for God's ownership" (Is. 43:21; Eph. 1:12; 2:10; 3:10). We can see the same truth in connection with the dedication of the priests of the Old Testament. Then, too, we observe the use of the word as applied to our Lord in a well-known passage, "I sanctify Myself" (John 17:19), meaning "I consecrate myself." It is, therefore, important and essential to remember, as one of the foundations of our life and experience, that the root idea of sanctification is consecration. We are redeemed to be set apart, dedicated, consecrated, "kept for the Master's use."

Then, as a result, sanctification comes to mean "purification," or a true condition before God. This is the natural and necessary consequence of our possession by God. Scripture proceeds from etymology to usage and goes on to show the moral and ethical meaning of our being consecrated, or separated. To be used when set apart involves fitness, and Scripture speaks of a twofold fitness, meetness. We are first of all made "partakers of the inheritance of the saints in the light" (Col. 1:12). Then, as the outcome of this, we are made "useful for the Master" (2 Tim. 2:21). When God possesses us we are possessed by His presence, and the Holy Spirit cannot be in us without purifying our thoughts, desires, and motives and so equipping us for His service.

Thus sanctification primarily refers to the act and fact of belonging to God, and then as the outcome, the proof of this in the life we live. This is how it has been put by one writer:

> Wherever one finds in the Bible "holy" or its cognates, whether in the Old Testament or the New, whether in the Psalms or Wisdom Literature or Gospels, the meaning is everywhere fundamentally the same. God as God only is holy in the absolute sense, for He alone possesses the perfection of moral being. They who belong to God by self-dedication belong to Himself also in moral likeness for they share His life.[1]

The Place of Sanctification

It will help us to understand the meaning and importance of sanctification if we consider it in relation to its place in Paul's teaching in Romans, chapters 1 to 8. In

[1] Swete, H. B., *The Study of the English Bible*, p. 214.

1:18 to 3:20 the Apostle shows that man's unrighteousness demanded divine righteousness; then, from 3:21 to 4:25 he points out how God provided this righteousness in Christ and how it is to be received by faith; and then in 5:1–12 he shows how the righteousness lasts in spite of every obstacle. Up to this point he has been concerned only with these three great truths but now at once comes an important question. If this righteousness thus covers the past and guarantees the future, what about the present in between? This is the problem of chapters 6 to 8, dealing with sanctification. Since righteousness as justification is salvation from the penalty of sin, so righteousness as sanctification is salvation from the power of sin, and this, with a brief reference to glorification as salvation from the presence of sin, is the great theme of chapters 6 to 8.

It is important to remember that the believer has been set apart for God through Christ's redemption from the very outset by the "offering of the body of Jesus Christ once for all" (Heb. 10:10). In this sense, all who believe are "saints," or sanctified from the moment of their acceptance of Christ (Col. 1:12–13). The Holy Spirit bears witness to this: "For by one offering He has perfected forever those who are being sanctified. And the Holy Spirit also witnesses to us" (Heb. 10:14–15). All believers are, therefore, said to be "sanctified by God the Father, and preserved in Jesus Christ" (Jude 1). To this effect we read in Paul's epistle to the Corinthians, "To the church of God which is at Corinth, to those who are sanctified in Christ Jesus, called to be saints" (1 Cor. 1:2). This refers to the Christian's position and, of course, in no way depends upon his spiritual condition at any moment, for the weakest, most ignorant believer has this relationship.

SANCTIFICATION

We know that among these Corinthians there were contentions, there was pride in human wisdom, they were described as "carnal" and still "babes in Christ," they were "puffed up," and they were sadly indifferent to sin in the church. Yet the Apostle says of these very people, "You were sanctified" (1 Cor. 6:11); and in the same letter he speaks of them as possessing the indwelling of the Holy Spirit (1 Cor. 3:16). It is thus clear that a sanctified person is one who belongs to God, whose position in Christ is settled quite apart from anything that he himself is or does. Everyone who believes on the Lord Jesus Christ is in Christ, has been sanctified by the offering of Jesus Christ once and for all, and as such is truly a "saint" in position. He grows *in* grace, rather than into it. But it is, of course, essential that our position should become expressed in our personal experience.

The Apostle divides men into three classes. Some he calls "natural," not having the Spirit (1 Cor. 2:14). This refers to men who have not been born again and are, therefore, neither justified nor sanctified. Others are described as "carnal" believers, who walk after the flesh, those who are babes in Christ when they ought to be growing into Christian manhood (1 Cor. 3:1–4). Yet, notwithstanding this weakness, these believers are included among those who are called "saints" at the outset of the epistle. The third class is "spiritual," which refers to the man who is walking in the Holy Spirit in fellowship with God in Christ. The believer is intended to become more and more thoroughly separated unto God, consecrated, dedicated in heart and life, and more and more conformed to the image of his Master. This is the meaning of "growth in grace." The believer is not only to be free, as in justification, from the penalty of sin but also free from the power, the bondage, the dominion of it. This is a pathway for the whole of the Christian life, and it is sometimes described as "progressive sanctification." It is clearly taught by the Apostle in such a passage as 2 Corinthians 3:17–18. This process goes on to the close of the believer's life on earth (Eph. 5:25–26) and will be completed when the Lord Himself appears (Eph. 5:27; see also Phil. 3:20–21).

This, then, is the place and force of sanctification in the Christian life. It refers exclusively to one who is already saved and who is desirous of being delivered from the power and control of sin, as well as from its penalty, and made more and more Godlike. This state requires a man to realize, first of all, his position in Christ and God's purpose concerning him, and then to be conscious that God requires what He has purposed. Thereby sanctification is seen to be the logical and inevitable outcome of justification.

The Provision for Sanctification

It will again help us to understand Paul's teaching in Romans 6–8, if we consider the divine provision for our becoming holy. The Apostle leads up to it by a question (Rom. 6:1). Someone is assumed to object to his teaching on justification and to ask: "Does not this doctrine of righteousness by faith encourage to sin?" The Apostle answers by showing that the death of Christ has two results: (1) it meets a guilty past, and (2) it also meets a sinful present. It thus deals not only with sins (plural) but also with sin (singular), not only with the fruit but also with the root. Sin is death, disease, and departure; righteousness must meet all three aspects. In Romans 3:21

SANCTIFICATION

to 5:11, the main thought is of sin as death; in 5:12 to 8:39, of sin as disease. In chapters 12 to 16 the ruling idea is of sin as departure. Thus the Apostle deals with justification, sanctification, and consecration.

Now let us observe by a careful study of the general teaching of Romans 6–8 what provision God has made for our sanctification. It is assumed, first of all, that the person to be sanctified is already justified, according to the teaching of 3:21–26 and 4:5. Then comes the needed provision for the sin that still dwells in the believer. The subject is introduced generally in 5:12–21 by the contrast instituted between Adam and Christ. Through Adam we have become involved in sin and death, and through Christ we are involved in righteousness and life. Then in chapter 6 is shown the Christian's relation to sin. First comes the teaching that continuance in sin is utterly impossible (verses 1–14). This is due to the fact that the believer has union with Christ in His death and life. This does not refer to personal experience but to actual fact as accomplished by Christ. It is this that gives force to the first key word of the passage, "Do you not *know?*" As Christ's death changes our relation to God and provides for our justification, or legal discharge, so it also is intended to change our character. It does this by means of a spiritual union with Christ. Herein lies the force of the second key word, the important word *reckon* (verse 11), which means "to count upon a thing as true." When Christ died we are reckoned by God as having died with Him, and when He rose again we are regarded as having risen. This reckoning of God is to be met by a corresponding reckoning on our part, and we are to believe concerning Christ what God teaches us has actually taken place. Thus when it is realized that we are spiritually united with

GRACE AND POWER

Christ in His death and life, justification by faith is shown to involve no license to sin.

Then the Apostle goes on to teach with equal clearness that continuance in acts of sinning is equally impossible (verses 15–23). This is shown by the thought of subjection to Christ as a Master, together with the contrast between the old life and the new. In the past we were slaves to sin; in the present we are servants to holiness. It follows that the old master and the old service are absolutely impossible. It is at this point that the third key word of the chapter is vital and important, *present* (verse 19). As we have reckoned ourselves dead to sin and alive unto God, we are to surrender ourselves to Him as those who are alive from the dead, and every faculty of our being is to be presented to Him for His use and service. Thus justification by faith is seen to be an introduction and an incentive to holiness. While the Christian has liberty from sin, he has no license to sin. It is particularly important to note that Romans 6:14 sums up the entire subject of these three chapters, "Sin shall not have dominion over you, for you are not under law, but under grace." "Sin shall not have dominion over you": this is the teaching of chapter 6. "You are not under law": this is the teaching, as we shall see, of chapter 7. "But under grace": this is the teaching of chapter 8.

Then follows the important and essential question of the relation of the Christian to law (chap. 7). In this connection it is necessary to remember that law stands here for self-effort, the endeavor of self by its own unaided powers to do the will of God. Up to the present the Apostle has taught that the grace of God in the death and resurrection of Christ provides for victory over sin. But now he has to deal with the experience of struggles against indwelling sin. The problem may be stated thus: if the believer need not and ought not to sin (chap. 6), can he not, nevertheless, make himself holy? The answer is a very decided negative and is shown in two main lines of teaching. In the first place, the old life is seen to be fruitless, and the new life alone fruitful (verses 1–6). The Apostle's argument proceeds along the line of the illustration of marriage, and without going into the details of his treatment, the threefold thought is perfectly clear: union, fruit, service. This is intended to teach the result of our union with Christ in His death and life; and just as he had spoken of "newness of life" (6:4), so now he emphasizes "newness of the Spirit" (7:6). Then, in an important passage (Rom. 7:7–25), he goes on to show that the believer cannot possibly sanctify himself by effort of his own. Law may order, but it cannot effect; it commands but does not equip; it condemns but does not enable. The struggles within cannot possibly bring about holiness, because of the fact and power of indwelling sin. Thus, as a man contemplates himself in his efforts to be holy, he is necessarily led to utter despair (verse 24). Hence, just as the Apostle had previously taught that man by no effort of his own can justify himself (chap. 3), so now, with equal clearness, he teaches that man cannot sanctify himself (chap. 7). At this point, however, it is necessary to guard against a misconception. The terrible struggle depicted in chapter 7 is not to be understood as giving an excuse for sin, for this chapter does not depict the normal Christian life, which is one of victory. The struggle here described cannot possibly make sinning inevitable, or else no real conquest and no real holiness would be possible. We shall see this as we study the next chapter.

The last and most important aspect of the present

subject is the Christian's relation to divine grace, as brought out in chapter 8. The Apostle has already stated that the believer is "under grace" (6:14), and in this chapter it is shown what the grace does. Christ's redemption, while it covers the past, does not leave the present unprotected, and it is, therefore, wrong to say that the Christian cannot help sinning. A scholarly writer, Adolf Deissmann, says that the original meaning of the word rendered "condemnation" (8:1) refers to civil *disability* and means there was no legal embarrassment that could therefore be conveyed from one person to another.[2] This has been aptly rendered into the language of spiritual experience by Harrington C. Lees who translates the word by "handicap," so that the verse will read: "There is, therefore, now no 'handicap' to them that are in Christ Jesus." It is of vital importance that this should be seen, experienced, and enjoyed. Just as chapter 7 teaches the impossibility of holiness in man's way, so chapter 8 is equally clear about the possibility of holiness in God's way. And as in chapter 7 "I" occurs thirty-three times, without a single reference to the Holy Spirit, so in chapter 8 there are no less than twenty references to the Holy Spirit and practically none referring to ourselves. It is impossible, and for our present purpose unnecessary, to outline the whole of the teaching of the chapter, but it will be worthwhile to look generally at what the Apostle teaches. If special attention be given to the first four verses, as in some respects the heart of the teaching, every disability or "handicap" will be seen to be more than met by the divine provision. The disability of the flesh through sin is met by the power of the Spirit (verses 1–11). The disability of the heart through fear is met by the presence of the Spirit (verses 12–17a). The

2. Deissmann, Adolf, *Bible Studies*, p. 264.

SANCTIFICATION

disability of circumstances through persecution is met by the peace of the Holy Spirit (verses 17b–30). And the disability of life through opposition is met by the possession of the Holy Spirit (verses 31–39).

The Apostle shows that righteousness in Christ means victory over sin (chap. 6), that this victory is impossible by any effort of self which is powerless for holiness (chap. 7), and that this is blessedly possible in and through the Spirit, who equips, assures, and triumphs in and for us over the flesh, over sufferings, and over opposition (chap. 8).

Now we are able to understand what the Apostle means by the believer's being "free from sin." He uses this term in three places, and each time in a different sense. First of all, there is freedom from the *penalty* of sin (Rom. 6:7). This is the judicial act of God in justifying the repentant and believing sinner. It does not refer to a moral change of heart but simply to the act and fact of God's accounting the believer as righteous in Christ and therefore released from the penalty of sin by reason of what Christ has done. Then comes the thought of freedom from the *practice* of sin, by a change of service (6:17–18). The believer is regarded as having left the service of one master for that of another, and under the new Master there is no possibility of any claim on the part of the old but, on the contrary, a new service in the practice of righteousness (6:20–22). Then, lastly, comes the thought of freedom from the *power* of sin (8:2). A mightier force has entered into the life of the believer, that of the Holy Spirit, which, having set him free from the dominion of sin, enables him to fulfill the will of God and do that which is right and true. And thus the righteous requirements of the law are fulfilled in him who walks not after "the flesh," but after "the Spirit" (8:4). This is the teaching found elsewhere, when the Apostle says, "Walk in the Spirit, and you shall not fulfill the lust of the flesh" (Gal. 5:16). It is this presence and power of the Holy Spirit within the heart that, in spite of the presence of indwelling sin, assures the soul of victory. There is, perhaps, no passage more important for this purpose than one that is often misread through failure to see the precise point of the original, "The flesh lusts against the Spirit, and the Spirit against the flesh; and these are contrary to one another, so that you do not do the things that you wish" (Gal. 5:17). It is the presence of the Holy Spirit that prevents the believer from doing the evil that he would do otherwise, because the law of the Spirit of life in Christ Jesus gives him the victory over the law of sin and death.

All this gives special point to the question often asked today, whether sinning is inevitable to a believer. Must Christians sin? The answer is, "No, certainly not." This is the teaching of the apostle John, for he says: "These things I write to you, that you may not sin. And if anyone sins, we have an Advocate with the Father, Jesus Christ the righteous" (1 John 2:1). If, therefore, this means what it says, it indicates that he wrote that epistle, with all its wonderful depth and wealth of teaching, for the very purpose of showing Christians how they might live without sinning.

The question of the relation of the believer to sin is one of very great importance; indeed, it is scarcely possible to exaggerate the momentous issues that spring from a true conception of what the Bible teaches on the subject. It will simplify matters if we limit ourselves at this point almost entirely to the teaching of the First Epistle of John, especially because there is so much in that part of God's

SANCTIFICATION

Word that bears on the matter. The Christian life is intended to be one of continual safety.

It is a subject that needs careful study and, therefore, careful handling, but we shall be perfectly safe if we proceed along the line of God's Word, neither going in front nor dropping behind. First of all, it is essential to study every passage in the epistle where the word *sin* occurs: chapter 1:7, "sin"; 1:8, "no sin"; 1:9, "sins"; 1:10, "not sinned"; 2:1, "not sin"; 3:8, "sins"; 3:9, "cannot sin." It is only when we look at all these passages that we are in a position, by induction, to arrive at the truth concerning our relation to sin. We find that there is a clear distinction to be kept in mind between "sin" and "sins," between the root and the fruit, between the principle and the practice. We observe this as we study three verses: "If we say that we have no sin" (1:8). To "have sin" is to possess the principle. "If we say that we have not sinned" (1:10). To "sin" is to express that principle in practice. Now notice, "If anyone sins" (2:1). There is an alteration from the "we" of 1:8 and 10 to the "anyone" of 2:1. Possibly the Apostle rather shrank from saying, "if we sin," because the ideal of the Christian life is sinlessness. What that sinlessness means we shall see presently, but we must notice that there are parallel words, and three lines of teaching:

> If we say we have no sin
> If we say we have not sinned
> If anyone sins

The reference to the Christian is perfectly clear; and "if anyone sins" shows that even a saint may sin. But if the saint should sin—mark that—"We have an Advocate with the Father." There is a perfect propitiation provided: "If anyone sins, we have an Advocate." There is no allowance for sin, but a perfect provision in case we do sin; no need to sin, no right to sin, no compromise with sin, no license, but a provision in case we do. On board ship the provision of life belts and lifeboats is not associated with any intention to have a shipwreck, but they are there in case of need. When it is said here, "If anyone sins, we have an Advocate," it is the provision in case of need. There are two Advocates. The Lord Jesus Christ is the Advocate with the Father, and the same word is used of the Holy Spirit by John in his gospel—He is the Advocate within (John 14:16, Greek). We have Christ's perfect provision *for* us, and the Holy Spirit's perfect provision *in* us.

There are three views about the relation of sin to the believer, and the believer to sin, which have a special bearing on our life. Two of them are wrong; one is right. By the use of the ordinary terms we may see what these three views mean.

The first is often called *eradication* and means "the removal of the sinful principle within." Now, this goes too far; it goes beyond Scripture, and it is contrary to experience. "If we say that we have no sin, we deceive ourselves" (1 John 1:8), but we do not deceive anybody else. Ask anyone who teaches eradication this question—a question that goes to the very basis of the whole matter—"Do you believe in the perpetual need of the Atonement to cover any defect from the moment of supposed eradication? Is the Atonement necessary for the rest of your life?" "Certainly" is the answer. To which the reply is obvious: "Then you are a sinner." As long as we need the Atone-

SANCTIFICATION

ment there is sin, whether in defect or otherwise. For we must never forget that sinlessness is not merely the absence of sinning; it is the presence of the complete and perfect will of God fulfilled in our life, and to mention this is to see at once the need of the atoning sacrifice to the very end of our days.

The second view is called by the term *suppression*. Now, if eradication goes too far, this does not go far enough, because suppression emphasizes fighting and struggling that will almost inevitably land us in defeat again and again. This is the error of those who think Romans 7 depicts the normal Christian life. Romans 8 begins with "no condemnation," and it closes with "no separation." But between the two there is "no defeat." This is the true and proper Christian experience. Suppression, therefore, is inadequate, miserably inadequate, to the truth of God.

The real word and the real thing is *counteraction*. Not eradication—that goes too far; not suppression—that does not go far enough; but counteraction, which just expresses the truth. "The law of the Spirit of life in Christ Jesus has made me free from the law of sin and death" (Rom. 8:2). There are two laws, and just as gravitation can be counteracted by volition, the higher law of the will, so the lower law of sin and death can be counteracted by the presence of the Holy Spirit in our hearts. That is why, as we have seen, in Romans 7 there are about thirty occasions where we find "I," "I," "I," with no reference to the Holy Spirit, while in Romans 8 we get all those references to the Holy Spirit and almost nothing about "I," "I." It is the law of counteraction.

A little girl, so it is said, was once asked by her teacher: "What did Paul mean by the words, 'I keep under my body' (1 Cor. 9:27, KJV)? How did he do it?" Her answer was, "By keeping his soul on top"—that is the law of counteraction. We must not dream that the sinful principle is eradicated, and we must not trouble about suppressing it. We must allow the Holy Spirit to come into our life and reign supreme in the throne room of the will, so that there may be this constant, continuous, blessed, and increasing counteraction. That is the word, or something like it, that Paul had in mind when he said in Romans 6:6, "Our old man [our unregenerate self] was crucified with Him, that the body of sin might be done away with [not destroyed or annihilated]." The Greek word used, *katargeo*, always means "to rob of power," "to render inoperative," "to put out of employment," "to place among the unemployed." This is why Paul always stopped short of eradication and yet was never content with suppression. This is what is meant by saying that our life is a life of continual safety.

Some of us say every Sunday, "Vouchsafe, O Lord, to keep us this day without sin." This is the teaching of counteraction. "Grant that this day we fall into no sin." This is the law of counteraction. "That we may perfectly love Thee, and worthily magnify Thy holy name." How marvelously those old writers knew the secret of holiness! So the Christian, while he continues to have the principle of sin in him, need not and ought not to express that principle in practice. But if he does, there is a provision, "Jesus Christ the righteous." Not Jesus Christ the loving, or the merciful, but "the righteous." Christ deals with us on a righteous level and treats the sins of His people by a righteous principle. He has no favorites and makes no qualifications or allowances. Sin is sin, whether in God's people or not. The provision is there in case we should need it.

The Practice of Sanctification

In view of all that has been said, it becomes a very practical and definite question as to how this sanctification can be realized. What is its method? How is this provision to be made part of the personal life of the believer? To this question there are two answers, according as we consider one or the other aspect.

The divine side. The apostle Paul speaks of our being "sanctified in Christ" (1 Cor. 1:2). He also says that Christ is made for us "righteousness, sanctification and redemption" (1 Cor. 1:30). These three truths sum up the whole of the believer's life and of Christ's relation to him. The one gift of God is the person of Christ who is, from different aspects, our righteousness in regard to the past, our sanctification in regard to the present, and our redemption in regard to the future. He is our sanctification. A complete work in this respect has been wrought for us by Him; as complete as our justification, "Sanctified through the offering of the body of Jesus Christ once for all" (Heb. 10:10). Christ is our sanctification, the Holy Spirit is our sanctifier, and we are the sanctified. The possession of Christ as Savior and sanctification is made real to us by the Holy Spirit, who glorifies Christ to our souls according as we need Him.

The human side. The Holy Spirit does His work through the Word of God, "Sanctify them by Your truth. Your word is truth" (John 17:17); "And for their sakes I sanctify Myself, that they also may be sanctified by the truth" (John 17:19). The truth of God is the great instrument used by the Spirit. Through this we obtain at once a knowledge of sin, of salvation, of sonship, of the indwelling of the Spirit, and of the real value and power of the sacrifice of Christ. Paul's emphasis in his great chapter on sanctification is on *knowledge*, "Do you not know" (see Rom 6:3, 6, 9, 16; 7:1). This thought of the truth of God in relation to our sanctification is found in a number of passages in the New Testament, and they all teach the same lesson: "You are already clean because of the word" (John 15:3); "The washing of water by the word" (Eph. 5:26); "Since you have purified your souls in obeying the truth" (1 Pet. 1:22).

Associated with the Word of God is faith, which is our response to the divine revelation. Faith appropriates Christ for sanctification just as it did for justification. This is the meaning of Paul's words, "sanctified by faith" (Acts 26:18). We can also see the same truth if we consider the force of the Apostle's "as" and "so," "As you have therefore received Christ Jesus the Lord, so walk in Him" (Col. 2:6). How did we receive Christ? By faith. Even so we are to walk—by faith. As there are four factors at conversion, so there are four in the Christian life—the Lord, the Spirit, the Word, and faith. Faith, as an act, receives Christ for justification. Faith, as an attitude, appropriates Christ for sanctification. The Lord provides for us a new relationship and also a new nature, and these two together sum up the meaning of righteousness. This holy nature is a gift bestowed on our souls by the Holy Spirit, and it is accepted and maintained by faith. Then in turn will come the graces of love and hope. Faith looks up to the living

SANCTIFICATION

Lord; love looks around on those for whom He died; and hope looks on to the coming of our great God and Savior. Thus the whole Christian life, past, present, and future, is realized by the believer.

An error very prevalent among uninstructed Christians, and one to be guarded against constantly, is that of practically assuming that Christ is to be accepted by faith and then maintained only by fighting—just as if Christianity were pardon by the Savior's free gift and purification by the believer's constant struggling. On the contrary, it is both justification and sanctification in the one Lord, and both are to be appropriated and maintained by faith. Holiness is not an achievement but a gift, and in the acceptance, appropriation, enjoyment, and use of the gift will be found our growing sanctification. Sanctification is first and fundamentally a position in which we have been placed in Christ by His redemption, and in which we are to realize experimentally all that is involved in what He has done. Christ is all—pardoning, justifying, sanctifying; and faith means surrendering, yielding, dedicating, trusting, using, obeying. The Christian life from first to last is the Christ-life and a life of faith.

It is significant that almost everything is associated with faith. We are "justified by faith" (Rom. 3:28; 5:1) and saved by faith (Eph. 2:8). We "live by faith" (Gal. 2:20); we have "access [to God] by faith" (Rom. 5:2); "we walk by faith" (2 Cor. 5:7); our hearts are "purified by faith" (Acts 15:9); we overcome by faith (1 John 5:4); and we receive the Holy Spirit by faith (Gal. 3:14). When the soul learns this lesson of the all-embracing nature and necessity of faith, it has become possessed of the true secret of Christian living. Faith receives Christ, rests on Him, reckons on His faithfulness, and realizes His presence.

GRACE AND POWER

Faith appropriates divine grace, applies it to momentary need, appreciates its value, and abides in it every moment. It is of no wonder that the Apostle lays such stress on the life of faith in the great chapter known as "the roll call of faith" (Heb. 11), by saying that "without faith it is impossible to please Him" (verse 6).

IV
CONSECRATION

We have already seen something of the meaning of justification and sanctification. Justification is the divine provision of a new position for the soul in Christ, involving a new relationship. Sanctification is the divine provision of a new condition for the soul through Christ, involving a new fellowship. The connection between the two is found in regeneration, understood as the divine gift of new life in Christ that expresses itself in the new birth of the Spirit.

We have observed that both justification and sanctification are complete in Christ when viewed from the divine standpoint, for Christ as the wisdom of God is made to us righteousness (or justification) for the past, sanctification for the present, and redemption for the future (1 Cor. 1:30). But the realization of their results in personal experience and spiritual blessing is often gradual. Justification is complete and eternal and admits of no degrees; we are not more or less justified but "justified from all things" at once and forever. This is so, quite apart from our experience of it. Sanctification, too, in the sense of God's having separated us for Himself is equally complete in His intention and purpose, but the realization of it in our lives is gradual and progressive. The act by which we accept this divine position, purpose, and provision develops into an attitude, a process, a progress. We obtain in order to maintain, retain, and attain. At this point is seen the New Testament distinction between consecration as God's separation of us for Himself, and as involving the consequent purification of soul necessary for His use of us. The latter is included in the former and arises out of it. Because God marks us as His own, He prepares us for His service by conforming us to the image of His Son. It is to this truth of the gradual and progressive maintenance, retention, and attainment that we must now address ourselves.

When the matter of justification is settled and sanctification is realized as the will of God for the believer (1 Thess. 4:3), the question at once arises, How can this will of God be done? How can the life of sanctification be lived? The one answer, and that both fundamental and inclusive, is, By the realization of our true and abiding relation to God and our position before Him as not only redeemed from sin but also redeemed for God's possession and service. In the realization, acceptance, and maintenance of this position will be found one of the secrets of power and blessing in the spiritual life. It must be considered from the divine and human standpoints.

The Divine Requirement

We can see this very clearly in Romans 14:9. Let us face it carefully and definitely. "To this end Christ died and rose and lived again, that He might be Lord." This means "that He might be Lord" of our lives, Master of our entire existence. The "absolute monarchy" of Jesus Christ

CONSECRATION

is the one condition of genuine Christian living. We have the same truth in Colossians 1:18: "He is the head... that in all things He may have the pre-eminence." Consider also 1 Peter 4:11, "That in all things God may be glorified." And note that Paul's most frequent and fullest title for our Savior is "the Lord Jesus Christ," or "Jesus Christ our Lord." Let us therefore settle it once and for all and then realize it continuously, "We are the Lord's" (Rom. 14:8).

The Old Testament affords unmistakable illustrations of this great truth. We remember that Israel was a redeemed people, delivered out of Egypt, but delivered from Egypt in order to belong to God forever. They were brought out and brought in, saved to serve. We notice in Leviticus, chapter 1, that the first offering named is the burnt offering, and as this offering means not propitiation but consecration, it is sometimes wondered why we have it first of all and not, instead, the sin offering. But we must remember that all five offerings were for the people of God, for believers and not for the unconverted. The people of Israel were already God's people on the basis of the Passover sacrifice of redemption. When this is realized, the place and meaning of the burnt offering become clear. It is the logical, immediate, and necessary outcome of a redeemed position, and as the offering was entirely consumed by fire, so was the life of the offerer to be wholly the Lord's. We have the New Testament counterpart of all this in exact and beautiful sequence in the epistle to the Romans. In chapter 3, we see the great propitiation whereby we are brought nigh to God, forgiven, justified. In chapter 6, we have our identification with Christ in His death and life. Then in chapter 12 comes the burnt offering, the "living sacrifice" which is our "logical" service (see Greek). It is the "logical" outcome of those "mercies of God" by which we are redeemed (verses 1 and 2).

Another notable illustration of this truth is found in the story of Joshua (5:13–15). Israel had been redeemed, and after the long wanderings and backsliding of their life in the wilderness, they were again in covenant with God on redemption ground (Josh. 5:2–11). The ordinances of the covenant were once more fulfilled and the old position resumed. What was now needed? They required a new revelation, a new and distinct lesson, a fresh and definite step. But what was this? Not the revelation of God as redeemer; they had that in Egypt. Not the revelation of God as teacher; they had that at Sinai. What was really necessary was the revelation of God as Lord and Master. And this is exactly what was given: "As Commander of the army of the Lord have I now come" (Josh. 5:14). He was there not merely to assist Israel against the Canaanites, not simply to second Joshua's efforts, but to take charge, to assume full command, to be Commander, Master, Lord.

The practical power of this truth is evident. It is the secret of peace in Christian experience and of ever-increasing peace in proportion as the lordship of Christ is realized. In Isaiah 9:7 it is first government, then peace. If the government be upon His shoulder, peace will be the immediate and constant result. It is also the source of power. "Our wills are ours to make them Thine," and in the absolute monarchy of Jesus Christ is power for character and conduct. Just as the riots in Trafalgar Square, London, many years ago were quelled by the assertion of the rights of the Crown to that area, so the assertion and acceptance of the "crown rights" of Christ will give peace

CONSECRATION

and power to the Christian life. Holiness is "wholeness" and is intended to apply to each faculty of our being, body, mind, feeling, imagination, conscience, will—everything.

> That all my powers with all their might
> In Thy sole glory may unite.

Into every part of our life, inward and outward, this lordship of Christ is intended to enter, and when it does, it is the guarantee of blessing. This, then, is the divine requirement, absolute, imperative, universal.

The Human Response

All God's revelation is conditioned upon human acceptance for full realization and enjoyment. This is so at every stage. Christ as Savior is only realized by the acceptance of faith, and in the aspect now before us it is necessary for us to respond to the claim of God upon our lives.

The first part of the response may be stated in the word *receive*. It is one of the great words of the New Testament. "As many as received Him" (John 1:12). Believers "receive abundance of grace" (Rom. 5:17). All through the New Testament much is made of our receiving, welcoming into our lives God's full provision in Christ. "As you have therefore received Christ Jesus the Lord" (Col. 2:6). It means the acceptance, appropriation, and application of Christ by faith for all our need.

The second part of the response may be expressed by the word *realize*. *Knowing* is one of the great key words of holiness (Rom. 6:3, 6, 16; 7:1; 1 Cor. 3:16; 5:6; 6:2, 3, 9,

15–16, 19; 9:24). This knowledge is intended to cover the fact, nature, and effect of sin; the fact, character, and power of salvation; the fact, meaning, and force of our union with Christ in His death and resurrection; and the fact, force, and blessedness of the Holy Spirit dwelling in us. Holiness very largely depends on a full knowledge and a full assurance of our position and provision in Christ. Our position is that we were slaves of Satan and sin, but we have been redeemed by the blood of Christ. These are facts undeniable and unalterable. But they carry with them the inevitable consequence that we belong to Him who has paid the price; we are His property, His possession. He is first our Savior and then our Lord, our Master, our Disposer. This position and possession involve and ensure perfect provision, and our knowledge includes this: "That we might know the things that have been freely given to us by God" (1 Cor. 2:12). We must realize all this and accept it in its definiteness, certainty, and blessedness. Then we shall have taken the second step toward holiness.

From this reception and realization we proceed to the next step that can best be stated in the apostolic word *reckon* (Rom. 6:11). This is another of the practical words of holiness. It is a "metaphor taken from accounts." It means we are to regard as true all that God says about Christ and about our position in Christ. We are to account as belonging to us all that Christ has done by His death and resurrection, to reckon, literally, this as our own. When He died, we died; when He was buried, we were buried; when He rose, we rose; when He ascended, we ascended. We are absolutely one with Him and are to regard ourselves as so united to Him that all the benefits and blessings of His redemptive work shall become ours in practical reality. So that when temptation to sin comes,

CONSECRATION

we at once reckon ourselves dead to it and it will have no power over us; when the call to purity and obedience is heard, we reckon ourselves alive in and with Christ to it, and the power at once comes. Thus, reckoning, that is, continually depending on and appropriating Christ, we find the "innumerable benefits" of His redemption becoming ours and the result is holiness.

Then we come to the next step that may be expressed by the word *surrender*. In Romans 6 we have it in the word *present*. We are called first to present ourselves to God (verse 13), and as a consequence, to present our members as weapons of righteousness for God and as "slaves of righteousness" with a view to holiness (verse 19). The same attitude and word are found in Romans 12:1, *present*. It denotes one definite act of surrender, presentation, committal of ourselves to God as those who are His, and who wish to show, in daily experience, that this is so.

The last stage of our response is found in the word *abide* (John 15:4). This means the maintenance of our realized position, the act becoming an attitude, the initial presentation being continued in one long, constant attitude of full dedication. "And now, little children, abide in Him" (1 John 2:28). This means "Stay where you are." This will include abiding in Christ's word (John 8:31), abiding in His love (John 15:9), abiding in Christ Himself (John 15:4–7), abiding with God (1 Cor. 7:24). It means that we simply continue as we have begun, never drawing back, never retreating, but letting God's fact of consecration become a constant factor by means of a life of dedication. "You are my God" is to be followed by "I am Your servant" (Ps. 143:10, 12). Then we shall learn the secret and enjoy the blessedness of the only true Christian life. If we thus "admit" Christ as Lord, "submit" to Him in everything, "commit" everything to Him, and "permit" Him to be everything, and to do all His will in us, then we shall indeed "transmit" His life and grace to others, and all that we are and have and do shall be to the glory and praise of God.

PART II

Protection for the Christian Life

"Sin shall not have dominion over you."—*Rom. 6:14*
"Rich to all who call upon Him."—*Rom. 10:12*
"So that you come short in no gift."—*1 Cor. 1:7*
"Sincere and without offense till the day of Christ."—*Phil. 1:10*

V

MEDITATION

The spiritual life which becomes ours, and is constantly realized by means of justification, sanctification, and consecration, must be maintained and sustained if it is to grow and increase in vigor, power, and blessing. Spiritual life in the true sense of the term is far more than spiritual existence; it implies strength, vigor, progress, joy, and satisfaction. "I have come that they may have life, and that they may have it more abundantly" (John 10:10). This abundant life is the only life that will really influence others and fully realize the will of God.

For the maintenance of spiritual life certain conditions are necessary. As with physical life, so with spiritual life, we have to use means and fulfill requirements, and this not intermittently but as the habit of our life. It is with the chief means or methods that we shall be concerned in this and the following chapters. Taking an illustration from the body, let us bear in mind that for the maintenance of life we require good food, pure air, and regular exercise. To the first of these we now turn our attention, when we speak of meditation. The good food is, of course, the food of the Word of God, for as food builds up the tissues of the body, repairs damage, and preserves us in health, so the Word of God is the complete food of the soul. It is noteworthy that we have it brought before us in the Bible as milk for babes (1 Pet. 2:2; 1 Cor. 3:2), as strong meat for adults (Heb. 5:14), affording us the necessary constituents of spiritual nutrition, and as honey (Ps. 19:10) suggesting the pleasure and enjoyment of dessert in addition to the food actually necessary for life and work (Jer. 15:16).

Coming now more closely to the details of this important element of spiritual life, we notice its subjects, its character, its outcome, and its times.

The Subjects of Meditation

One of these is the Word of God, that revelation of God's will which is enshrined in the Old and New Testament Scriptures. The counsel to Joshua emphasized this (Josh. 1:8), and the description of the truly blessed man makes meditation a prominent feature (Pss. 1, 2, and 3). The great Bible psalm (119) has at least seven references to meditation, while the value and necessity of the Word of God to the godly life are the outstanding features of the whole psalm. Let it be clearly and constantly borne in mind that true Christian living is not possible apart from meditation on the Word of God.

Meditation is also to be exercised on the works of God. The psalmist realized the value of this form of meditation (Pss. 77:12 and 143:5). The works of God in creation, the actions and activities of God in history and general providence, the dealing of God in our own experience and in particular providences are all fit subjects for meditation and should all have their place in our thought and life.

But above and beyond all, our meditation should be

MEDITATION

centered upon God Himself. "May my meditation be sweet to Him" (Ps. 104:34). "I will meditate on You" (Ps. 63:6). Our use of God's Word and God's works is only intended to lead us up to the consideration and contemplation of God Himself, and on Him we must ever fix our gaze. God first, God everywhere, is the secret of the "highest" Christian life.

It is important to notice that meditation is nowhere associated with ourselves, or our sin, as the subjects. Such an attitude of introspection would be as unhealthy as it would prove discouraging and disheartening. To be occupied with ourselves is dangerous; to be occupied with our sin is depressing, for we cannot fathom either the treachery and deceitfulness of our hearts or gauge the depths of our depravity. But if our hearts are led out from themselves and fastened on God, then "in [His] light we see light" (Ps. 36:9) on ourselves and see ourselves as we really are, while the same gaze will also lead us to the secret of grace and blessing in God Himself. It is sometimes said, "For one look at self, take ten looks at Christ." But why not take eleven looks at Christ and none at self? It might be infinitely more profitable.

The Character of Meditation

How shall we meditate? What does it mean?

It must be an individual and personal meditation. Let us look well and long at this text, made as clear as the printer's art can emphasize its teaching: "My meditation... to Him" (Ps. 104:34). Do we see the point? "My" meditation, not someone else's. The great, the primary, the essential point is firsthand meditation of God's Word as the secret of Christian living. Remember Dr. Andrew Murray's definition of milk as "food that has passed through the digestion of another." And so all the little books of devotion, the helps to holiness, the series of manuals of thought and teaching, including these very lines, represent food that has passed through the spiritual digestion of others before it comes to us and has to be used as such. Do we then decry all these? God forbid; we establish them, but only in their place and for their purpose. If they are put first, to the exclusion of the Bible alone, and the Bible day by day, they become dangerous and disastrous, crutches that prevent vigorous exercise and inevitably lead to spiritual senility. If they are put second, they can become delightful and helpful, inspirations to further thought and suggestions of deeper blessings. When we have had our own meditation of the Word, we are the better able to enjoy what God teaches us through others of His children, especially those whom God honors with special gifts of teaching. So it must be first, foremost, and constantly, "My meditation."

Meditation must be real. It must be "the meditation of my heart" (Ps. 49:3), and "the heart" in the Scripture means the center of the moral being, including the intellect, the emotions, and the will. It implies that we come to the Word to be searched thoroughly, guided definitely, and strengthened effectually. It is not a time for dreamy, vague imaginings, but for living, actual blessing, whether in the form of guidance, warning, comfort, or counsel.

Meditation will also be practical. What are its stages or elements? *First*, the careful reading of the particular passage or subject, thinking over its real and original meaning. *Second*, a hearty turning of it into prayer for mercy and grace that its teaching may become part of my life. *Third*,

MEDITATION

a sincere transfusion of it into a resolution that my life shall reproduce it. *Fourth,* a wholehearted surrender to, and trust in, God for power to practice it forthwith and constantly throughout the day. It is to be noted that the word *meditate,* in our English version, represents two Hebrew words—one meaning to "muse" or "think," and the other implying "speech," or audible thinking (see Ps. 5:1). These two elements should always be blended; thinking over the Word, its meaning, its application, its message, and then talking to God about it, in confession of past failures, in prayer for future blessing, in fellowship in present joys or needs. Thus will meditation become so practical, so vital, so blessed that we shall find in it our chief joy and our indispensable daily power for service.

The Outcome of Meditation

We have necessarily anticipated this in some degree, but let us note more definitely a threefold result of meditation.

The first is *spiritual strength.* When we study carefully the description of the blessed man in Psalm 1, we see very clearly his spiritual strength by reason of his meditation. He is like the tree as contrasted with the chaff—steadfast and dependable, because he is rooted in the strength of God. Why did John say the young men were strong? Because the Word of God was abiding in them (1 John 2:12–14). When do none of the steps of the righteous slide? When the law of God is in the heart (Ps. 37:31). When do we not sin against God? When His Word is hidden in our hearts (Ps. 119:11).

Then comes *spiritual success.* Twice at least is "prosperity" associated with meditation of God's Word (Josh. 1:8–9; Ps. 1:2–3). And even if we translate "do wisely," instead of "prosper," we get the same idea, for it is abundantly evident from the New Testament that spiritual wisdom and perception come from the knowledge of God's Word and fellowship with Him (Phil. 1:9–10; Col. 1:9). All Christian experience testifies to blessing, power, and prosperity in spiritual life and service in exact proportion to meditation on the Word of God.

Not least is *spiritual satisfaction.* "How sweet are Your words to my taste" (Ps. 119:103).

The physical enjoyment of food and dessert is but a faint illustration of the joy of the Word in the heart. "Your words were found, and I ate them,/And Your word was to me the joy and rejoicing of my heart" (Jer. 15:16). "I rejoice at Your word/As one who finds great treasure" (Ps. 119:162). If we look at the titles of the Scriptures given in Psalm 119, such as ordinances, statutes, judgments, we see they are words that, as a rule, we associate with what is dry and dull and uninteresting! Yet these very statutes were a delight, a joy, a supreme satisfaction to the psalmist, and so it ever is if our hearts are right with God. "How precious also are Your thoughts to me, O God!" (Ps. 139:17).

The Times of Meditation

There is, of course, a sense in which our thoughts should ever be turning to God and His truth. "Oh, how I love Your law! It is my meditation all the day" (Ps. 119:97). The attitude of our souls, if in a healthy state, will ever tend to the recollection of God whenever the opportunity occurs.

MEDITATION

But this attitude is only possible by means of stated times for meditation. These are the occasions for providing fuel for daily use. There can be no doubt that early morning is the very best time for this. The body is rested, the brain is free and unencumbered; hence the receptive powers are more available. It may not be possible to spend much time; but let no one be discouraged because of this, for *quality* is the *desideratum,* and that can be put into even five minutes. Let the attempt be made with five minutes on a single text, or phrase of a text, and the exercise will soon justify itself, and a hunger will spring up for five minutes more! And it will soon be found how marvelously we are able to do without that extra five minutes' sleep! Let but the time, long or short, be well spent, and the fruit will be quick to appear and lasting in effect.

Another time mentioned in the Scripture is eventide (Gen. 24:63), that time of twilight, "'twixt the lights," which often brings a quiet moment or two to many a life. When the toil of the day is approaching its close, or is over, or between the work of the afternoon and evening duties, there often steal over the soul a sense of God's nearness and a peace of heart that tell of the Spirit's presence. Then is the time for dropping the book or paper, and for allowing the soul to listen to God and to speak to Him. If our circumstances allow it and, like Isaac, we can go "into the field" for our meditation, there will be an added delight, as in the quiet of the gathering shadows, broken only by the rustling of trees or the evensong of the birds, we stand face to face with God and allow His Word to have "free course" in us and "be glorified."

Once more, night is often an opportunity for meditation (Ps. 63:6), and if it be so, let us use it well. Before retiring to rest, let the heart be bathed in the water of the Word (Eph. 5:26), and then if "in the night we sleepless lie," the Word will "heavenly thoughts supply." In any case, however, and whatever our circumstances, we must find time, make time, and take time for this blessed exercise of meditation. It is marvelous how easy is that apparently impossible task of *making time*.

It is hardly possible to exaggerate the importance of the meditation on Scripture for the maintenance and progress of the spiritual life. The Bible enters into every part of our experience, because it is the revelation of God on which our life is necessarily based and to which it should make a constant response. For this reason no life can be either safe or strong that does not put meditation on Scripture in the forefront. It should be with us as with the psalmist, "I thought about my ways, and turned my feet to Your testimonies" (Ps. 119:59), and with the prophet, "Your words were found, and I ate them,/And Your word was to me the joy and rejoicing of my heart;/For I am called by Your name,/O Lord God of hosts" (Jer. 15:16).

Our contact with the Word of God will thus be an exact test of our discipleship and character. The Bible is the mirror in which we see ourselves as we are and as God sees us, and it must be evident that if we never use, or rarely use, the mirror we cannot be sure of our real state before God. Christianity is largely a matter of the condition of soul, stress is laid on character, and character is power. Now, character needs solitude for growth; solitude is "the mother country of the strong"; but solitude without the Bible tends toward morbidity, while with the Bible it is a guarantee of vitality and vigor.

Let us, then, be sure that amid the hurry, flurry, scurry, and worry of life we "take time to be holy" by means of

MEDITATION

meditation on God in His Word. Let not even Christian work rob us of this secret of true service and blessing. Let the superficiality of many lives warn us "to give attention to reading," to meditate on these things, "that our profiting may appear to all," and also glorify God. Like the psalmist, let us be able to *remember* past seasons of blessed meditation (Ps. 119:23), to *realize* present seasons of equally blessed privilege (Ps. 119:97), and to *resolve* that the future shall also be full of such seasons of life and health and joy (Ps. 119:15).

VI
PRAYER

In addition to good, suitable, and regular food, the body requires a pure atmosphere in order to have a healthy and vigorous life. In like manner the spiritual life must have both the food of God's Word and the pure atmosphere of prayer if it is to be thoroughly healthy, strong, and true. We are now to consider some of the aspects of prayer as the "Christian's vital breath" and "native air."

The illustration of breathing may help to introduce a subject that fills so prominent a part in the revelation of God's will. Breathing is the function of a natural, healthy life. It is a spontaneous, unconscious, incessant act and habit, and it marks the person as in normal health and vigor. So, also, if the spiritual life is healthy, prayer will be the natural, spontaneous, and unceasing expression of it. This is what the Apostle spoke of as "continuing steadfastly in prayer" (Rom. 12:12).

We may therefore be sure that the emphasis laid upon continual prayer in the Word of God and the prominence given to it in the lives of all the most eminent Christians in all ages are two sure tokens of its absolute necessity for every believer.

CONTINUANCE IN PRAYER—WHAT IT MEANS

The word translated "continuing" in prayer (Rom. 12:12, and Col. 4:2) is used in several connections that illustrate its meaning in prayer. It is used of the little boat that waited on our Lord continually (Mark 3:9); of the apostles giving themselves to their ministry (Acts 6:4); of the disciples on the day of Pentecost (Acts 2:42); of Simon Magus remaining with Philip (Acts 8:13). It includes the ideas of "clinging closely to and remaining constant in" and implies continuous devotion expressed in steadfastness and earnestness.

It means, therefore, very much more than frequently recurring times of prayer. This is to water down the true idea; for the thought is of an attitude rather than an act, even though it is frequently performed. Prayer is something vastly beyond the utterance of words; it is the relation and constant attitude of the soul to God.

This attitude toward God consists of several elements, chief among them being submission, desire, trust, fellowship. There is first and foremost the submission of the soul to God, the attitude of surrender whereby we are in harmony with the will of God. Then there is the desire of the soul for God, the aspiration and longing for His presence and grace. "So pants my soul for You, O God. My soul thirsts for God, for the living God" (Ps. 42:1–2). Then comes the confidence of the soul in God, the sense of dependence on Him, and the utter distrust of self and our own will and way. Last of all there is the fellowship of the soul with God, the delight in His presence and freedom of communication with Him at all times.

This is something of the meaning of continuance in

prayer, and it can be easily seen that this may be at times quite independent of words. It is the soul's realization of God and one's deep, quiet joy in His presence and grace.

Continuance in Prayer—What It Does

It makes God's *presence real*. This presence brings *peace*, which calms the soul in the presence of dangers. It brings *joy*, which cheers the soul in the pathway of difficulty and duty. It brings *glory*, which sheds a radiance on ordinary life and illuminates the commonest tasks with the light of heaven.

It makes God's *power manifest*. The heart is thereby garrisoned against sin. There is nothing like continuance in prayer to keep us from sin. The soul is thereby armed against temptation, for the life of prayer surrounds us with divine power. The life is thus protected against leakage. God's power seals up the crevices and preserves the spiritual life intact.

It makes God's *will clear*. By a life of prayer the perceptions of the soul are clarified. By it the moral powers of the soul are kept balanced. By it the determining powers are strengthened and rendered vigorous, and decisions are more easily and safely made. Thereby we have preservation from error at any critical moment, because through a life of prayer we learn to understand the providence and guidance of God much more clearly and are enabled to "perceive and know what things we ought to do, and have grace and power faithfully to fulfill the same." There is, as it were, an accumulation of grace and power in the ordinary life that makes us ready for all emergencies.

It makes God's *service easy*. Through continuance in

prayer we are "strengthened with all might, according to His glorious power" (Col. 1:11) for all necessary service. God's calls are readily met because we are prepared, "ready for every good work" (Titus 3:1). And His service is seen to be perfect freedom, "whom to serve is to reign" (*cui servire est regnare*), and we learn to realize in blessed experience that His yoke is indeed easy and His burden light.

Continuance in Prayer—What It Needs

We must honor the Holy Spirit of God. The Spirit of God is the source, the atmosphere, the power of prayer. He is the "Spirit of grace and supplication." Three times He is very clearly associated with prayer (Rom. 8:26–27; Eph. 6:18; Jude 20), and we must honor Him definitely and constantly if we would know the secret of a life of prayer.

We must meditate on the Word of God. The food of the Scriptures, God's revelation of His will, is needed to sustain prayer. The promises are to elicit prayer. The Word and prayer always go together, and no prayer is of use that is not based on, warranted by, and saturated with the Word of God.

We must include prayer for others. True prayer cannot be limited to our own needs. As the soul learns more of God's will and purpose, it enlarges itself and goes out in love and pity for all the souls for whom Christ died. Intercession is not only a definite but also a very prominent part of the real Christian life (1 Sam. 12:23). Our priesthood means intercession. Our Lord's work has intercession for its crowning point (Rom. 8:34; Heb. 7:25). The Holy Spirit intercedes. We, too, must pray for others, and in so praying our own life of prayer will be fully realized.

We must have special occasions for prayer. The life is fed by these. The attitude is based upon acts. The life of the body depends on separate and successive acts, whether of breathing or eating, and so it is with the soul. These times of prayer are the storage, the reservoir of daily power and progress.

The best times for this are undoubtedly morning and evening, and of these two morning is by far the more important. A few moments at midday are also of immense help. But whenever it is, we *must* have and, if necessary, make time for prayer.

Let us then begin at once, starting with but five minutes and not attempting too much at first. The five will soon grow to six, seven, eight, ten, and even more. The habit will come to be a delight. It will prove as strange and impossible to omit it as our regular meals. God's presence will be more and more a delight; God's power will more and more be felt; God's blessing will more and more be realized in all our influence and service.

VII
FAITHFULNESS

Five times in the New Testament Christians are compared to "babes" or "children" (1 Cor. 3; 1 Cor. 14; Eph. 4; Heb. 5; and 1 Pet. 2), a term that normally indicates the commencement and early stages of Christian life. But there is this great difference between them. The first, third, and fifth refer to the beginning of the Christian life, to the need of growth, and of not remaining children. The second and fourth partake of the nature of warnings, though there is a significant difference between the point of the warning in each case. In 1 Corinthians 14 an appeal is made to the Corinthian churches not to "become" children in their mental life, though they are to continue babes, innocent, childlike, in regard to evil. In Hebrews 5:12 they are warned on the ground that they had once made progress but had reverted to spiritual babyhood. This is worse than childhood; it is second childhood. It is not immaturity but dotage, not juvenility but senility. And it is to warn and safeguard them that the writer uses such plain terms. He says he cannot teach them high, deep, full, rich truths, such as that of the priesthood of Christ (verse 11) because of their state of spiritual dotage.

There are thus four classes of Christians: "babes," growing Christians, mature or full-grown Christians, and invalids.

GRACE AND POWER

If we study 1 John 2:12–14, we shall see the first three classes described. If we wish to avoid becoming Christians of the fourth class, we shall do well to ponder the passage in Hebrews 5 and apply its truths rigidly to our own lives as we consider the solemn truth of spiritual degeneration.

Spiritual Degeneration Is Possible

God's will for us is progress: "Grow in grace" (2 Pet. 3:18); "Let us be borne on to maturity" (Greek of Heb. 6:1). Progress is always in relation to the will of God, which is to be increasingly known, accepted, obeyed, loved, and enjoyed. The Old and New Testaments teem with commands, encouragements, entreaties, and warnings on this subject. Conversion is but the start; what is also needed is continuance. The book of Daniel states, "Daniel continued" (1:21) and "Daniel prospered" (6:28). "If you abide" (John 8:31), "continue in the faith" (Col. 1:23), and "patient continuance" (Rom. 2:7) are other phrases indicating the need for continuance.

The body makes progress almost spontaneously, as it were, though even this is according to law. The progress of mind and soul, however, is not so apparently spontaneous but is dependent upon the will and upon the constant and strenuous observance of definite laws of training. Yet it must be borne in mind that spiritual progress does not mean primarily intellectual power of achievement, but increased spiritual capacity and deeper experience, a more tender conscience, a more fully surrendered will. In reference to these elements God's message is, "Go forward."

God's will for us is often not fulfilled. The growth is stunted, the capacity contracted, the life hindered through

FAITHFULNESS

lack of progress. The main characteristic of this is an inability to discern between good and evil, between good and better, between good and best (Phil. 1:9–10). The Hebrew Christians are described as "dull of hearing" (Heb. 5:11) and "unskilled" (Heb. 5:13). This does not mean that the soul ever becomes unregenerate again, but it certainly means that it becomes *de*generate.

What are the causes of this backsliding and degeneration? Sometimes it is due to worldliness which, like a bad atmosphere, penetrates, lowers the temperature, and chokes the vitality. There are not a few sad instances of this spirit influencing earnest Christians. "You ran well. Who hindered you?" (Gal. 5:7). Sometimes the trouble is due to what may be called "weariness," a spiritual and moral sluggishness which does not wish to go forward, an inertness which tends to sap the vigor and spiritual buoyancy. Sometimes, however, the cause is willfulness, some secret sin which leads to unfaithfulness and tends to eat away the spiritual life. As a rule this degeneration does not occur all at once. As the old Latin proverb says, "No one suddenly becomes base." Like a great tree which, though gradually affected by fungi, may topple over at once in some storm of wind, so a spiritual life may be infected by error and evil silently and secretly for a long time, and then in a moment of special testing and strong temptation, a catastrophe occurs. Let us, then, write it on heart and mind and conscience that spiritual degeneration is possible.

Spiritual Degeneration Is Sinful

God gives us full opportunity to grow. "Though by this time you ought to be teachers, you need someone to teach you" (Heb. 5:12). The time since their conversion was so long that these Christians ought to have grown wonderfully since then. To use Dr. Andrew Murray's illustration, a babe of three months is a beautiful picture, natural and delightful, but a babe of twenty years would be a monstrosity. If a person had come to the age of manhood and still possessed only the body and brain of a babe, how terribly sad would the circumstances be. What, then, must God think and feel concerning those who have been "in Christ," born again for years, and are in spiritual experience only babes? May we not term them, without exaggeration, spiritual monstrosities?

The neglect of our opportunity for growth is sin. We cannot command growth, but we can hinder it, and it is this that constitutes our sin. There are Christians who are always talking of their preference for the "simple gospel," and they believe they are showing their faithfulness and humility, when all unconsciously, but very really, they are testifying to their own unfaithfulness and laziness. Those who speak of wishing for nothing save "Christ and Him crucified" must not forget that in that very chapter (1 Cor. 2) Paul goes on to say, "However, we speak wisdom among those who are mature" Christians. The fact is that "Christ crucified" covers the whole Christian life from grace to glory and is concerned not only with the simplest but also with the deepest truths. It is a mark of immaturity to be content with that which is perfectly obvious without thought and trouble. Immaturity is sin if we are neglecting opportunities of ripeness and power. The call is clear not to continue to lay spiritual foundations, that is, to be content with elementary truths (see Heb. 6:1).

FAITHFULNESS

SPIRITUAL DEGENERATION IS HARMFUL

It is harmful *to ourselves*. We become dull or heavy or sluggish of hearing. We have no spiritual digestion but must perforce be content with the plainest fare (Heb. 5:11–14). And with dull perceptions and weak powers of assimilation we are a prey to the microbes of temptation that are powerless against the vigor of health. We are liable to contract the malaria of worldliness and all other dangers attendant on a low state of health. In the East a gentleman once wished to test the truth of the statement that the sheep will not follow a stranger, and the shepherd told him that only the sick sheep would respond to his call. And he found it to be true. What a lesson is this! Who are the people that go here and there, accept this or that newest fad in teaching, go astray into error and sin? The sick sheep. Those who do not know how to discern between good and evil and are a prey to every deceiver.

It is harmful *to others*. "By this time" since conversion such "babes" "ought to be teachers," but instead of this they still need to be taught their spiritual alphabet. They ought to be feeding others, instead of being themselves fed. Churches remain nurseries when they ought to be training grounds. What a loss to others this means! The majority of Christians are silent, leaving all teaching to a few, with the result that only a little work is done, and the neighborhoods of their churches are not evangelized. "You ought to be teachers." They ought to have the knowledge to enable them, the interest to incite them, and the loyalty to compel them to be helpers of others. Oh! the unutterable sadness of the little work done when so much more could be done with the actually existing number of Christian people.

GRACE AND POWER

Spiritual Degeneration Is Remediable

How? We must start from the foundations but not stay there. Axioms in mathematics are necessary foundations, but no one dreams of simply going on learning them. They are to be used. We commence all education by learning the alphabet, but we do not limit ourselves to this process; we use the letters! The old masters had only the primary colors of red, blue, and yellow, but how marvelous were the combinations "by reason of use." So must it be in the Christian life. In one sense we must "leave" the rudiments and "go on" to ripeness. It is "by reason of use" (Heb. 5:14) that we grow and make progress. Just as in learning a foreign tongue we must have daily practice, setting the same brain cells in vibration every day, just as a pianist needs constant practice if the joints are to be kept flexible and supple and the execution become more proficient, so the believer needs "use," exercise, training, if he is to "go on to perfection" (Heb. 6:1). What is this "use"?

There must be the atmosphere of prayer. There must be the daily exercise of prayer and intercession. Daily appearing before God and realizing the spiritual perception, spiritual enlargement, and spiritual power that come from waiting on God.

There must be the use of good food, the daily exercise of study and meditation, daily feeding on the Word of God, and this never allowed to be intermittent.

There must be activity, the daily action of trust, love, obedience, and hope. Trust in the real presence of our God and Father. Love to Christ and to others in Him. Obedience to every known command of God's Word. Hope in Him whose coming is our "blessed hope." And all

FAITHFULNESS

this daily, hourly, momentarily, until it becomes the very fiber of our being.

This is the exercise or "use" of our spiritual faculties, and the result will be that we shall never degenerate but go forward from strength to strength. Thus, living in the atmosphere of prayer, feeding on the food of the Word, and exercising ourselves in practical living in and for God, we shall know what the true Christian life really is in its continual growth, its exultant joy, its spiritual power, its blessed usefulness, its deepening peace, its widening influence, and its unceasing witness to the grace and glory of God.

VIII

OBEDIENCE

No one who has once understood what the Christian life means can ever be the same again. Either he will be better for his knowledge, or else he will be worse. His life cannot possibly be lived on the same original plane of spiritual experience. If, by means of this knowledge, we obtain ideals and do not at once set to work to realize them, both the ideal and the real will be lowered from that time forward. Hence the importance, the necessity, of taking heed to such a message as that which was given by our Lord to His disciples: "If you know these things, happy are you if you do them" (John 13:17).

The Christian Life Starts with Knowledge

"If you know these things." It is absolutely essential that we should know these things. A knowledge of Christian truth is of paramount importance, of primary necessity. It does matter what we believe. Knowledge is ever one of the springs and sources of action. "Conduct," as Matthew Arnold said, may be "three-fourths of life," but the other fourth is the motive-power of the three. A train is much longer than the engine, but the engine provides the motive-power. A building is much larger than the foundation, but the foundation is very necessary. A tree is much wider than the root, but it is the root that gives life to the tree. Knowledge is absolutely necessary.

It is necessary in the Christian life for *protection*. If we knew more, we should be preserved from error on this or that side. In the later epistles of Paul, in which we have the mature spiritual experience of the apostle, we find a strong emphasis on *knowledge*, and in almost every case the word so rendered refers to mature, ripe knowledge. These epistles are full of the thought of knowledge as the mark of a growing Christian, a ripening spiritual perception, a deepening knowledge of God's truth. In the still later epistles, the Pastorals, we have the phrase again and again, "sound doctrine," not so much in the sense of intellectual clearness as of healthful doctrine, that which ministers to spiritual health. In the last epistle of Peter (which consists of only three chapters) we have, again, this thought of mature knowledge. In almost every case in which the word occurs in those chapters it is a rendering of the word *epignosis*, and the epistle closes with "grow in the grace and knowledge of our Lord and Savior Jesus Christ." Then, again, in the First Epistle of John, the key note is "that you may know." Knowledge will keep us from error of all kinds. A clear conception and perception of Christian truth will be our greatest protection. It is worthwhile to notice the three stages of the Christian life mentioned in the First Epistle of John (2:12–14). The little children are those who *have*, the young men are those who *are*, and the fathers are those who *know*.

Not only for protection, but also for *peace*, knowledge is necessary. "I know whom I have believed and am persuaded that He is able to keep what I have committed to Him

OBEDIENCE

until that Day" (1 Tim. 1:12). That is the expression of the experience of a man who knows. As we look back over our past life, we may think of the things that we have read, understood, and learned. Every one of us has something to be included in this phrase, "If you know these things" (John 13:17). But it so happens there are at least five "things" in the immediate context that are essential elements in our knowledge. The first is, "He who is bathed" (John 13:10), he who has received the bath of a perfect justification. This is, as we have seen, at the root and foundation of all Christian living. We must have "the Lord our righteousness" for justification. Second, a perpetual cleansing. "If I do not wash you" (John 13:8). "You are clean, but not all" (John 13:10). This is one of the "these things" enforced in Scripture—perpetual cleansing in and through the Lord Jesus Christ. Third, loyal submission. "You call me Teacher and Lord, and you say well, for so I am. If I then, your Lord and Teacher" (John 13:13–14). Notice the two titles, Teacher and Lord. In the order of our experience it is Teacher and Lord; in the order of His purpose it is what He Himself claims—Lord and Teacher. We have been learning of Him as Teacher and what it is to call Him Lord. "To this end Christ died and rose and lived again that He might be Lord" (Rom. 14:9). Fourth, a lowly spirit. The Lord "girded Himself" and took the place of a servant, though filled with a divine consciousness: "Knowing... that He had come from God, and was going to God, He... took a towel and girded Himself" (John 13:3–4). In the very height of His divine consciousness, He stooped to the position of lowliness. Whenever we have been on the mountaintop and had a glimpse of divine things, we find we should have the same spirit of lowliness. Fifth, service to others. He not only took the position but also did the work of a servant in washing the disciples' feet.

"If you know these things." Do we know them? It cannot be too often emphasized that knowledge in the New Testament is not merely intellectual perception; it is spiritual experience. Do we know these things? Do we know all of these five? Do we know what it is to have Christ for our perfect justification? Do we know what it is to have Him as our continual sanctification? Do we know what it is to know Him as our Lord and Master and Teacher? Do we know what it is to have Him as our pattern of lowliness and service? Do we know these things? Christ *for* us our atoning sacrifice, Christ *in* us our living power, Christ *under* us our sure foundation, Christ *around* us our wall of fire, Christ *beside* us our perfect pattern, Christ *over* us our blessed Master, Christ *before* us our everlasting heritage.

THE CHRISTIAN LIFE PROCEEDS TO ACTION

"If you know these things, . . . do them." Christianity is not a creed alone; it is a life. If knowledge is the spring of action, action is the end of knowledge. Two words in the New Testament practically sum up all that is contained in the phrase "do them," *walk* and *work*. These may be stated as character and conduct, holiness and service. The "walk" comes first. We recall the frequency with which the word *walk* is used to express the activity and progress of the Christian life. Sometimes we find it in connection with sincerity; we are to walk before God (Gen. 17:1). Sometimes in connection with obedience; we are to walk after Him (Deut. 13:4). Sometimes in connection with

OBEDIENCE

union; we are to walk in Him (Col. 2:10). Sometimes in connection with fellowship; we are to walk with Him (Mal. 2:6). Perhaps this metaphor is used because walking is one of the three perfect forms of exercise, in which every faculty and power of our physical being is brought into play. There are forms of exercise quite as enjoyable that do not do this, but walking, running, and swimming do. The "walk" of the Christian life is intended to bring out every faculty of our spiritual being.

By "doing these things" we start with the act and then go on to habit and character. Many of us recall the teaching of Samuel Butler about passive impressions and active habits. We continually receive impressions, but if these passive impressions are not at once transformed into acts of the will, in order that they may become habits, then the impressions will have been in vain. If we are not already putting into practice in our wills, in our inmost being, what we know, we are already losing it. It is here that many of us fail in the Christian life, and fail again and again. Is it not simply terrible to think of failure when we might be going forward? Why is it terrible? Because if only we would at once translate, by means of the will, the impression we receive, we should get an influx of power and from the act would come a habit. Instead of our life being a series of intermittent acts, the acts would be joined to one another. This would not mean merely a chain but an ever stronger chain, one perfect line, forming at last the habit of our life. Then prayer would become easy, meditation on the Bible easy, making time for prayer and the Bible easy, surrender easy, obedience easy, because of the habit, the walk of life. There is something instinctive in the movement of the arm, or even of the body, in walking; and what that is in things physical, our spiritual life is intended to be, that we may be established, strengthened, settled.

And then will come work. Not merely character but conduct; not only holiness but service. Our Lord did something; He washed His disciples' feet, He served them in that moment of exalted consciousness. If we do not entertain the determination to work, our profession will be in vain. We have social and spiritual work to do. Wherever our life is treated in the New Testament we always find three aspects: eternal, internal, external—our relation to God, our relation to ourselves, and our relation to others. The fruit of the Spirit is ninefold—three with regard to God, three with regard to our fellows, and three with regard to ourselves (see Gal. 5). The threefold aspect of John's first epistle is clear and includes obedience to God, love to the brethren, and the possession of the Holy Spirit in the heart. When Paul preached to Festus, he preached righteousness, self-control, and judgment to come—our threefold relationship. So when we have been dealing with God it is natural that there may go forth from us to others the influence and power of a holy life and holy character in blessed and loving service.

There is, first of all, the home circle, and that may be for some of us the most difficult; but it must be faced. We have to "show piety at home." Let us, however, take care that the difficulties are not of our own making. Let the youngest of us remember that in the home life we are not infallible, even after we have had spiritual enlightenment. And we must see that those who are older than ourselves are not able to say, "Well, if that is what Christian living means, I do not feel drawn to it." We read in our Lord's life that "the house was filled with the fragrance" (John 12:3). So let it be with us in things spiritual.

OBEDIENCE

Then comes our church life. If we are in the ministry, we shall realize what the work of the ministry means in the light of the New Testament. But whether minister or layman, our work will mean devoted service for God, and loving and loyal service one for another, washing the disciples' feet. This is what we have to face. Somewhat quaintly, but very truly, three rules have been given for washing the disciples' feet. First, "the water must not be too hot." There is a danger of censoriousness, a serious risk of censoriousness in relation to others. If we scold, we shall scald, and that will be fatal. Second, "our own hands must be clean while we do it." If our hands are not clean when doing this work of washing the feet of others, this work of loving service, we shall not do our duty to our Master. Third, "we must be quite willing for others to wash our feet." This involves a good deal of humility. When these things are true of us, we shall have the true home and the true church life.

But it is necessary to look farther and to think not merely of the home life and of the church life but also of the national life. It is sometimes said that many Christians are indifferent to the thousand and one evils of the present day. Nothing could be more unfair than that charge. It cannot be forgotten that redemption and regeneration are never applied to society in the New Testament but only to the individual in regard to his spiritual needs; the gospel is primarily salvation, not civilization. But with this realized and kept before us, the gospel is to be applied to all life. It is our duty to apply the gospel to all the social ills of today. We face these social problems and bring to bear upon them the teaching of the New Testament. Nothing in this world can deal so quickly or so effectively with our social evils as the old-fashioned evangelical verities of the

New Testament. The problem of the unemployed can only be solved by Christian men and women, as also the problem of poverty, the problem of alcoholism, the problem of gambling, the problem of impurity, the problem of the desecration of the Lord's Day, and the problem of war. Not least of all is the problem of the use of money. Systematic and proportionate giving as the great New Testament principle ought to be applied by every one of us in every action of our life, in order that it may be seen that we are not forgetful of the social claims of others. Let us not forget, in this connection, that the Lord Jesus Christ does not look upon what we give but upon what we have left after we have given. Let us recall that while the Lord looked upon that widow's two mites (not one mite) He looked upon it because she had nothing left to give. When social problems are thus faced, none of them will prove insoluble.

But it is necessary to look farther still and think of the universal life, "If you know these things, happy are you if you do them." There is an application to evangelization. The home, the church, the nation, the world. This is in the line of God's will, and the Christian who puts world-wide evangelization in the proper place in his life—the first place, God's place—will find in it the key to everything in the home, in the parish, in the nation. "If you know these things... do them."

The Christian Life Culminates in Blessedness

"If you know these things, blessed are you if you do them." We shall know by experience the blessedness of holiness. This will involve the blessedness of spiritual

OBEDIENCE

peace, the blessedness of spiritual power, the blessedness of spiritual provision, the blessedness of spiritual permanence, the blessedness of "abiding." The joy of the Lord will be deep as we know Him as our righteousness for justification, our righteousness for sanctification, our righteousness for consecration.

Then there will be the blessedness of service! Is there any blessedness comparable with the blessedness of love? A man once went to his minister and asked him to tell him something about heaven, and the minister said, "Down the street is a widow with some small children. Go to the grocer—do not send but go; buy what you can from that grocer's shop; then go to the baker, then to the fruit store, and then take the things yourself, give them to this widow and pray with her."

The man did so, and in a little time he came back and said, "Pastor, I do not need to know anything now about heaven; I've been there!" He had realized something of the joy, the unspeakable joy of love! That is heaven, for "God is love."

Not least will come the blessedness of obedience. It will be the blessedness of putting into practice what we know, and it fills the soul with the peace of God in an ever-increasing degree.

And so we rejoice in the blessedness of work. Work will no longer be a toil but a joy; no longer a weariness but a delight. There is a hymn that we sometimes sing, "I've found a Friend," and it seems somewhat selfish, though we do not mean it for selfishness, when we sing those words in it:

> And now to work, to watch, to war,
> And then to rest for ever.

GRACE AND POWER

Would it not be better to sing,

> And now to work, to watch, to war,
> And then to *work* for ever.

It is of course true that "they rest from their labors," but it is also true that "they rest not day nor night"; to every healthy, vigorous Christian work is and ever will be the joy and delight of life.

What can we say of the blessedness of influence? This is the blessedness of realizing, in however small a degree and to however little an extent, the influence that is holy as it flows out from us to others. Some years ago a lady was walking home from the station about midnight after speaking at a large meeting in London. As she neared her home she thought she saw someone leaning against the wall, near the gateway of her house. She found that it was a young girl, and very soon she saw that the girl was ill. She took her in that night, gave her a bed, and everything possible for her comfort. The next morning she made arrangements for the girl to be taken to a suitable home where her needs would be attended to. But the end was very near. They telegraphed soon afterwards to the lady to come and see her. When she leaned over the bed to speak to the girl and spoke to her about better things, this is what the girl said: "I have not found it hard to think about God since I saw you!" Is there anything in this world higher than that—that people should not think it hard to think about God by reason of our life? "I have not found it hard to think about God since I saw you." "Blessed are you if you do them."

That is the life to which God is calling us, the life in

the home, in the church, in the nation, in the world. "Therefore, my beloved brethren, be steadfast, immovable, always abounding in the work of the Lord, knowing that your labor is not in vain in the Lord" (1 Cor. 15:58).

PART III

Possibility for the Christian Life

"The power of God to salvation."—*Rom. 1:16*

"His divine power has given to us all things that pertain to life and godliness."—*2 Pet. 1:3*

"How shall he not with Him also freely give us all things?"—*Rom. 8:32*

"That we might know the things that have been freely given to us by God."—*1 Cor. 2:12*

IX

KNOWLEDGE

This is pre-eminently a day of inquiry, of questioning as to fundamental principles. Some years ago, mainly under the guidance of the German scholar, Harnack, the question was rife, "What is Christianity?" Such questioning is natural and inevitable and ought to be heartily welcomed. The Jews were expected to tell their children the meaning of the Passover whenever the inquiry was made, "What do you mean by this service?" And the apostle Peter bids us to be ready to give a reason to everyone who asks why we are what we are (1 Pet. 3:15). In matters biblical, spiritual, and even ecclesiastical, it is essential for us to be able to explain and vindicate our position. One thing, however, we must never forget, that truth is many-sided. It is like a crystal with several faces rather than like a piece of glass with one flat surface. As a diamond with various facets, so truth has its different aspects; if only we realize this, we shall not go far wrong. Trouble arises if only one aspect is emphasized, for we are tempted to think that this is the only truth in existence.

During Christian history there have been, perhaps, three main periods in which emphasis has been largely placed upon certain aspects of truth. During the early centuries the chief emphasis was on Christ as the divine redeemer. In the sixteenth century the stress fell on Christ as the perfect justifier. During the nineteenth century the chief point seems to have been, as it still is, on Christ the complete deliverer. So that we have in the early centuries, "My Sin"; at the Reformation, "My Guilt"; and now, "My Weakness." The Christian life is concerned with the last of these three—My Weakness; Christ the complete deliverer. But, of course, the other two are presupposed. It is because Christ is the divine Savior, and because He is the perfect justifier, that we are enabled to contemplate Him as our complete deliverance from sin; and thus to consider our weakness, our bondage, our defilement, everything that touches the life of the believer in relation to sin. It will therefore be wise and well to look a little at the fundamental implications and presuppositions of the Christian life, in order that we may then proceed from stage to stage, from strength to strength, and from glory to glory.

This can best be done by concentrating attention on one of the numerous passages that reveal the believer's life in all the divine plenitude of grace and blessing: "At that day you will know that I am in My Father, and you in Me, and I in you" (John 14:20).

Our Strong Protection

"I am in My Father." This is the foundation, the relation of Christ to His Father. "What think ye of Christ?" is the question of questions today, and the union of the Lord Jesus Christ with His Father is the presupposition of everything. A book was published some time ago entitled *Jesus in the Nineteenth Century and After*. But we

KNOWLEDGE

have to think also of *Jesus in the First Century and Before*; this is where we must start.

Now, our strong protection, "I am in My Father," means this first of all: the Lord Jesus as the *revelation of truth*. He claimed to come from the Father, and He said He was the truth. He promised that the truth should make His disciples free. His constant word was, "I say unto you." This is the Lord Jesus Christ in His aspect as the prophet of God. Truth in the New Testament means two things, veracity and reality, and Christ is and reveals both.

But it also means the Lord Jesus Christ as *redeemer from sin*. He came not only to show but to save; not only to teach but to redeem. Sin has to be faced. We have to know what it is, and how it is to be removed. "God was in Christ reconciling the world to Himself" (2 Cor. 6:19).

This means, in the third place, the Lord Jesus Christ in His *rule over life*. He came preaching the kingdom of God, and by this is to be understood the reign of God over human hearts and lives. His claim was absolute over men. "Come unto Me," "learn of Me," "follow Me," "abide in Me"—these were His constant assertions and claims.

This is the idea found in old-fashioned theology: "Jesus my Prophet, Priest, and King." He is Prophet to reveal, Priest to redeem, King to rule. Here, then, is where we start—what I call our strong protection. This is what we think of the Lord Jesus Christ, and nothing short of this will satisfy either the New Testament teaching or the needs of any individual heart and life. In the introduction to a book by Sir Robert Anderson, the Bishop of Durham (Dr. Handley Moule) used these words, and they are worthy of constant repetition: "A Saviour not quite God is a bridge broken at the farther end."

GRACE AND POWER

OUR SAFE POSITION

"You in Me." After thinking of Christ as in the Father, we must consider ourselves as in Christ. "You in Me." We are in Christ, first of all, for *pardon*. Let us not be indifferent to these elementary truths. They are the presupposition of everything else. Pardon is the first blessing associated with the Christian religion. There is no other religion in the world that has this message of pardon. Professor Huxley once said: "There is no forgiveness in nature," and all the great writers of fiction for the last hundred years have had for their theme the nemesis of broken law. Kipling says somewhere:

> The sins ye do by two and two,
> Ye must pay for one by one.

Yet all through the ages we have been expressing our belief in the forgiveness of sins because we rest upon the revelation of the Lord Jesus Christ. His message of pardon makes forgiveness possible for everyone, perfect forgiveness, eternal forgiveness, assured forgiveness.

Then we are in Christ for *righteousness*. Righteousness is much more than pardon. Pardon is like being stripped of old clothes. Righteousness is like receiving new clothes instead. Pardon is negative. Righteousness is positive. A British monarch can bestow a royal pardon and manifest royal clemency to a man who is in prison, and when that man goes out, he is a free man, with the monarch's pardon. Yet as we see him going along the road, we know he is a pardoned criminal. What the king or queen of England cannot do is to reinstate the man as if he had never broken the law. To the end of his days he will be a pardoned criminal. But the Christian is not only a pardoned criminal, he is also a perfectly righteous man. What the monarch of England cannot do, the King of kings can do. That is the meaning of righteousness. An old woman once said, "It is too good to be true, but, praise the Lord, it is true!" We can heartily endorse that old woman's theology. We have righteousness, we are righteous in Christ, in the Lord who is our righteousness. That is what the apostle Paul meant in the well-known passage: "He made Him who knew no sin to be sin for us, that we might become the righteousness of God in Him" (2 Cor. 5:21).

We are in Christ for *peace*. If pardon is safety from condemnation and righteousness safety from guilt, peace is safety from fear. In some respects fear is the most terrible of all our daily experiences. Yet the new blessing of pardon and the new gift of righteousness will always issue in the new relationship of peace. First comes peace with God, and out of that "the peace of God" filling our souls. This is exactly what our Lord said: "These things I have spoken to you, that in Me you may have peace" (John 16:33).

On the day when Adam and Eve sinned there were three immediate results. The moment they sinned there was a consciousness of guilt. They knew they had done wrong. That was immediately followed by a sentence of condemnation. God condemned their sin. That in turn was followed by an act of separation. They were driven out of the Garden of Eden. Guilt; condemnation; separation. Now think of the gospel. At the end of Romans 8 the Apostle asks three questions: "Who shall bring a charge against God's elect?" (Rom. 8:33). There is no guilt. "Who is he who condemns?" (Rom. 8:34). There is no condemnation. "Who shall separate us from the love of

GRACE AND POWER

Christ?" (Rom. 8:35). There is no separation. The very three things we lost through sin we more than gain in Christ. This is our safe position, "You in Me."

OUR SURE PROVISION

"I in you." Christ in the Father is our protection; the believer in Christ is our position; and Christ in the believer is our provision. "I in you" is intended first of all for *life*. Christ provides more than pardon; He gives life. He provides more than peace; He bestows life. Our Lord Himself tells us this: "I am come that you might have life." All through the fourth Gospel the keynote of almost every chapter is life, until at length we have the purpose of the whole, "That you may believe that Jesus is the Christ, the Son of God, and that believing you may have life" (John 20:31). So that the highest gift is life, and this means Christ in the believer as his life, just as Paul said: "It is no longer I who live, but Christ lives in me" (Gal. 2:20). Let us take time to dwell upon this, and when we are alone, let us spend a moment and say to ourselves perhaps aloud, "Christ lives in me."

Christ is in us not only for life but also for *grace*. In the New Testament *grace* is one of the greatest words. It always means two things—God's favor and His blessing; His attitude and His action. We are told of grace to "help in time of need"; that grace is "sufficient"; that "God is able to make all grace abound." There are no two people alike. It is probable there is no experience that can be parallelled exactly by any other experience. Yet, whatever may be our personal need, our different hereditary tendencies, or our actual experience, God's grace is sufficient.

KNOWLEDGE

It is really only a false pride that would hide itself saying, "There is no life like mine, and my needs are too exceptional to be supplied!" Let us face Scripture when it says, "God is able to make all grace abound toward you, that you, always having all sufficiency in all things, have an abundance for every good work" (2 Cor. 9:8).

Then Christ is in the believer for *hope*. This points to the future. "Hope springs eternal in the human breast." Hope is one of the three Christian graces and a very prominent feature in New Testament Christianity. We find there not only faith and love but also hope. Hope is always associated with the coming of the Lord Jesus Christ. The reason people are not full of hope is because they are not concerned as they ought to be about the Lord's coming. In Scripture the Lord's coming is mentioned over three hundred times. This prominence shows its importance. Hope, in the New Testament, is never mere buoyancy of temperament but a Christian grace centered on the coming of the Lord. This is what we mean by Christ in us for hope. "Christ in you the hope of glory."

Our Satisfying Privilege

"You will know." What does this mean? To know, in the New Testament, is far more than something merely intellectual; it is that which may be called the verifying faculty, including mind, heart, conscience, and will. Knowledge in the New Testament is experience expressed in assurance. The text promises that we shall "know" the very three things mentioned.

"You will know that I am in My Father." There will be assurance in the believer's life that Christ is in the Father.

GRACE AND POWER

This comes through the Resurrection. From the time of the Resurrection onwards, Christ is never said to have raised Himself. It is always the act of God. The Resurrection was not Christ's own act but God's act in vindicating His Son, in bearing witness to what He thought about Christ. When the believer is assured that the Lord Jesus Christ is raised from the dead, he has the assurance that God did it, and that this is what God thinks of His beloved Son.

"You will know" also that the believer is in Christ. This comes through the death of Christ. We have the assurance that we are in Christ because of His death. That death in the New Testament always means these three things: substitution—"He died instead of me"; representation—"He died on behalf of me"; identification—"I died when He died." We cannot properly understand the Atonement unless we take all three together; and the assurance, "You will know that you are in Me," is the assurance that the death of Christ took place for our salvation and covers all our need.

Then there is the assurance that Christ is in us: "You will know that I am in you." This is associated with the life of Christ. We have the assurance that Christ is living. There is a story of a man looking at a picture of the Crucifixion in a shop window, and a little ragged urchin also was looking at it. The man pretended to know nothing about it and said to the boy, "What's that?" The boy, astonished, replied, "Don't you know that is Jesus on the cross who died?" And he told him the story of the Crucifixion. "Oh," said the gentleman, "is it?" and walked away. In a little while he heard footsteps coming after him. It was the little boy, and he said, "Sir, I wanted to tell you that He is alive!" Yes, this is the New Testament

KNOWLEDGE

perspective, "I am He who lives and was dead, and behold, I am alive forevermore" (Rev. 1:18). The assurance of Scripture is, "You will know that I am in you," the living Christ. So we have life and death and resurrection as the guarantee of our assurance in Christ.

This knowledge provides us with certainty. "You will know." Luke wrote his Gospel, "that you might know the certainty." Certainty is what everyone desires. "That you may know." There is so much uncertainty today. Someone has said that "mystery involves all spiritual truths." If this is so, it is not the mystery of vagueness and confusion but of truth's divinity and glory. It is not the mystery of fog but of sunshine, a mystery "dark with excess of light." The mystery is not in the truths but in those associated with them. A modern writer said that in the old days the prophets were absolutely certain and said, "Here I am," but nowadays the people say, "*Where* am I?" The New Testament has no such uncertainty. It has been acutely pointed out that there are two notes of modern life not found in the New Testament—wistfulness and pensiveness. There is nothing wistful and nothing pensive about New Testament Christianity: "I know," "I have," "I believe." "I am persuaded that He is able to keep what I have committed to Him until that day" (2 Tim. 1:12). It is usual to find out on enlistment a man's religious denomination. A soldier was once asked, "What is your persuasion?" He replied, "I am persuaded that nothing shall separate me from the love of Christ." Just so; and this is the assurance of the New Testament.

Our Spiritual Power

"In that day you will know" (John 14:20). What does this mean? "In that day"—we find the phrase three times in these chapters—once here, and twice in the sixteenth (verses 23, 26). "In that day" means, of course, the Christian dispensation, from the day of Pentecost onwards. "In that day" is in the day when the Holy Spirit should come. "You will know," and therefore all our Christian life is to be associated with the Holy Spirit.

The Holy Spirit is a *divine gift*. Pentecost was a kind of watershed. It looked back upon the time when the Lord Jesus was upon earth and looked forward to the time when the disciples would be influenced and empowered by the Lord Christ above. The Holy Spirit was the gift of the Father to the Son, and the Son shed forth that gift on the day of Pentecost. The Spirit of God was not given before, in that sense, because Jesus Christ was not yet glorified. It was necessary for Him to go up before the Holy Spirit could come down. But when He ascended and received the gift, He poured Him forth, and the divine Spirit has been with the church ever since. "In that day," therefore, means the whole of this dispensation, including the present moment.

From this comes the thought of the Holy Spirit as an *inward witness*. The Divine Gift of Pentecost becomes the inward possession of every individual believer who accepts the Lord Jesus Christ as his Savior; for, on believing, he is sealed with the Holy Spirit. The Holy Spirit becomes his, and at once the Holy Spirit begins to work in his soul and to give him assurance.

Then there is the Holy Spirit as an *outward power* in the life, significance Himself in character and service. This is the meaning of "in that day." Every gift in Christianity is associated with the Holy Spirit. This is the unique feature of the Christian religion, contrasted with which all other religions are as nothing. Other religions have their books,

KNOWLEDGE

their ethics, their philosophy, but not one of them has a Holy Spirit, as Christianity has,

> And every virtue we possess,
> And every victory won,
> And every thought of holiness—
> Are His alone.

This, then, is the New Testament life—these four things: perfect safety, perfect standing, perfect strength, and perfect satisfaction. Perfect safety—"saved by the LORD with an everlasting salvation" (Is. 45:17); perfect standing—"accepted in the Beloved" (Eph. 1:6); perfect strength—"strong in the Lord and in the power of His might" (Eph. 6:10); perfect satisfaction—"satisfied with favor, and full of the blessing of the LORD" (Deut. 33:23). Let us rest upon these, let us rejoice in them, because they are ours in Christ.

But now comes the question whether we "know" these things. Are they ours? Does anything hinder us from enjoying this Christianity? Shall we not ask ourselves this question? We have our needs and our difficulties, but God will meet and overcome our difficulties and satisfy all our needs, if we will just face this question and get right with Him.

There are perhaps only five possibilities in explanation of the reason why we do not enjoy our Christian religion. The first, and in some respects the greatest, is *sin*. Yet that need not trouble us, because "the blood of Jesus Christ... cleanses us from all sin" (John 1:7). The Lord Jesus Christ is able to deal with "sins" (Rom. 3:25) and also "sin" (Rom. 6:7)—the root of sin and its fruit in sins. He can deal with every one of them under all circumstances.

Second, it may not be sin, but *sorrow*. There are some who are weighed down with a burden of sorrow, sorrow in their hearts, sorrow in their homes, sorrow in their church, sorrow among their acquaintances—some sorrow that is terribly burdensome. To all such, God says, "Be of good cheer." A man wrote a postcard to a friend, and on that side of the postcard where it says "address only" he wrote the words, "Be of good cheer." When the friend received the postcard, he was compelled to pay extra postage and was not particularly pleased. He looked to see what the reason was, and on the "address" side he saw the words, "Be of good cheer," and underneath the postal authorities' stamp, "Contrary to regulation." There are many Christians who think that to be of good cheer is contrary to regulation. That is why they are doleful and sad. They look, as it has been said, as if their religion did not agree with them. Cheerfulness and smiles ought to belong to the Christian religion; these are *not* contrary to the regulations. "These things I have spoken to you, that My joy may remain in you, and that your joy may be full" (John 15:11).

Third, there are some people whom *circumstances* keep from enjoyment of religion. What are these? Just think of the word *circumstances*—those things that "stand around" us. But if they merely stand around they cannot keep out the sky. And so we must not trouble about things around us, but keep looking up. "Fear not; for I am with you: *look not around thee,* for I am thy God" (Is. 41:10, Hebrew). Circumstances should never overcome us. "How is Mrs. So-and-So?" "She is pretty well," was the reply, "under the circumstances." Then came the rejoinder, "What is she doing *under* the circumstances? The circumstances ought to be under her."

KNOWLEDGE

Fourth, someone says that it is *Satan*; not sin or sorrow or circumstances, but Satan. Yet Satan is a defeated foe. The Lord said, "The ruler of this world is coming, and he has nothing in Me" (John 14:30). And James said, "Resist the devil, and he will flee from you" (James 4:7). If we resist him, he will go. He can never overcome your individuality, and the grace of the Lord Jesus Christ is more than sufficient to meet every onslaught: "I give you the authority... over all the power of the enemy; and nothing shall by any means hurt you" (Luke 10:19).

Fifth, someone else says that it is due to *self*. That is, in many cases, the greatest trouble of all. Yet the Apostle says, "Not I, but Christ"; "Not I, but the grace of God that is with me"; "Not I, but the Lord." Three times over he says, "Not I, but..." If we face self in that way, self shall never have the victory.

"It is just as different as can be," said a young believer.

"What is so different?"

"Being a Christian. Everything is so different from what I expected."

"What did you expect?"

"When you used to talk to me about being a Christian, I used to say to myself, 'No, I cannot, for I shall have to do so many hard things, and I never can do them. If I become a Christian, I shall have to attend church and pray and read my Bible.' It is so different from what I thought."

"What do you mean? You go to church, and you pray, and you read your Bible."

"Yes, but then I love to do them. That makes all the difference. I love the Lord Jesus Christ, and therefore love to do all that He wishes me to do."

I once heard a friend say, "Faith makes all things

possible, and love makes all things easy." I would venture to add that hope makes all things bright. Here is Christianity. If you want to know how to become a Christian and enjoy Christianity to the fullest, it is all summed up in the little word *trust*. It means, first, the acceptance of God's Word; second, surrender to Christ; and third, the reception of His grace. In Ephesians 3:12 we find four words, and if we reverse them we get Christianity in the proper order: "In whom we have boldness and access with confidence through faith in Him." First faith, then confidence, then access, and then boldness; there we have the whole of the Christian life. That is the meaning of *trust*, of which we read so much in the New Testament. It means taking God at His word, surrendering to Him, receiving His grace and, of course, living in His presence.

Some will perhaps remember the story of the two friends of the great painter Turner. They visited him in order to see his pictures. When they arrived, Turner kept them for a short while in a closely shaded room before he sent the servant to take them up to the studio. In the studio, he apologized for his apparent rudeness by telling them that it was necessary for their eyes to be emptied of any glare before they could appreciate the colors in his pictures. We need to live in the presence of the Lord Jesus Christ, in order that we may be emptied of everything that is common and earthly, and in order also that we may see and rejoice in His beauty. Living with the Lord Jesus Christ, living a life of trust and fellowship will give us all this true Christian experience.

> Live every day with Jesus,
>   And tell Him everything;
> A life of richest blessing

KNOWLEDGE

Thy months and years will bring;
Tell Him thy aims and wishes,
　Tell Him thy hopes and fears;
The sunshine of His presence
　Illumines smiles and tears.

Live every day with Jesus;
　Let Him thy life control,
His voice of love inspiring
　Each impulse of the soul;
Lean on His word for guidance,
　Speak to Him of each grief,
Telling all things to Jesus
　Brings gladness and relief.

Live every day for Jesus;
　Oh, happy, restful lot!
His watchful care about thee;
　Never by Him forgot;
In darkest hour still with thee,
　In loneliest hour thy Friend,
Who never will forsake thee
　Unto thy journey's end.

And then? to live with Jesus
　In the full sunlight, where
No pain, or loss, or sorrow
　Will need thy trust and prayer;
But joy—His joy—forever
　Will crown His work of grace,
And thou shalt serve, beholding
　The glory of God's face.

—J.H.S.

X
POWER

The apostle Paul tells us the things that happened to Israel happened to them for examples or types and that the record was given for our admonition (1 Cor. 10:11). We are therefore justified in utilizing the history of Israel for spiritual purposes today. One important caution is necessary. We must bear in mind that whenever there are promises of future glory to Israel in the Old Testament, our use of those promises is spiritual and secondary, by way of application, and is not historical and primary, by way of interpretation. If we are not careful in this matter, we shall incur the somewhat cynical and yet true condemnation of those who take all the blessings to themselves and leave the curses to the Jews! For example, the chapter headings for Isaiah in some Bibles have much to answer for in this respect, because they take the promises to Israel and apply them to the church, with which primarily they have nothing whatever to do. But when we keep this truth clearly and constantly in mind, there is no reason why we should not use Old Testament passages with reference to our life today.

With this in view we may look at an Old Testament prophecy in Obadiah to learn from it the secrets of power for holiness: "On Mount Zion there shall be deliverance, and there shall be holiness; and the house of Jacob shall possess their possessions" (Obad. 17).

This prophecy seems to indicate some of the vital and fundamental realities associated with the Christian life. Israel is depicted as redeemed, restored to their former glory, after bondage to their terrible enemy, Edom. They are told that there will come a day when there shall be deliverance from their foe, a fresh consecration to God, and a recovery of all their possessions, as in the former time.

What do we understand by the Christian life? What are those blessings of which the Old and New Testaments are full?

SAFETY

"On Mount Zion there shall be deliverance." This is the foundation of everything—safety. The gospel starts here. The great New Testament word *salvation* means nothing more and nothing less, in the first place, than "safety," "deliverance," "escape from the *penalty* of sin." This is the first step into the Christian life; and it is well for us to ask this question, "Have I taken it?" It is altogether inaccurate to say that from time to time people have the second step in mind rather than the first. Yet we know it is utterly impossible to take a second step before we have taken the first, and holiness, a truer and purer and nobler life, is utterly impossible until and unless we have settled this first question—escape, deliverance, safety, from the penalty of sin.

Sometimes we speak of this theologically as justification. The word matters not; what is essential is the reality, the experience. So there comes to every one of us this question, "Am I safe? Am I delivered from the penalty of sin?" To which the true reply is, "There is therefore now no condemnation to those who are in Christ Jesus" (Rom. 8:1). It need hardly be said that the way of deliverance is the way of faith, the acceptance of Him who died that we might live, who by His death became our righteousness, "that we might become the righteousness of God in Him" (2 Cor. 5:21). This is the first and fundamental element of the Christian life, deliverance from the penalty of sin.

But, of course, deliverance goes on to refer to the *power* of sin—"those that escape," that is, those who are safe from the power of sin. This again, theologically, is sometimes spoken of—perhaps a little inaccurately—as sanctification; but it will serve for our present purpose—deliverance from the power of sin, whether that power is realized in connection with Satan, or with circumstances, or with self, our three spiritual foes. We read in John's first epistle and elsewhere of victory. This is the thought in connection with the prophecy of Obadiah—escape, deliverance, safety, in regard to the power of sin as it faces us today. Assuming that we have learned what it means to be delivered from the penalty of sin, assuming that we have learned what it means to have entered into that experience, we are to learn more of what deliverance from the power of sin means, the secret of victory over Satan, over the world, and over self. In Mount Zion there shall be safety.

Sanctity

"And there shall be holiness." It will be worthwhile to remind ourselves afresh of the fundamental conception of "holiness" in the Old and New Testaments. The root idea is always "separateness." Whether we take the Hebrew word or the Greek, whether we think of the English words connected with holy and holiness, or with saint, sanctification, and saintliness, the fundamental, basic thought is "separateness." There is an entirely different set of words connected with purification. Purification does not enter into the etymology of the word we translate as "sanctification," though the experience of purity is an essential and vital result and consequence. If we look at a passage such as Ephesians 5:26, we see that our Lord gave Himself for the church that He might sanctify, that is, separate it, "having purified it." There are other texts that clearly mark the distinction between the thought of sanctification and purification.

What do we mean by separateness? Negatively, we are to understand separateness from sin; positively, separateness unto God. "There shall be separateness," or "There shall be sanctity." That is one of the fundamental and predominant notes of the New Testament—separation *from*, separation *unto*. This is why places can be called holy. There was no moral virtue in any part of the tabernacle. It was not purer than any other place, but it was nevertheless called holy, because it was separated unto God. And so it was called a sacred place; because *sacred* has the same idea as *holy*—"cut off," "separated," "devoted." We read that Esau was a "profane person" (Heb. 12:16). Our modern idea of "profane" and "profanity" is very specific and has reference to one or two definite forms of evil. The original idea of "profane" is quite different. Outside every temple there was an enclosure that was perfectly public. It was called by the name of *pro fanum*, "before the fane," "before the temple." Everybody was allowed there; the ground was trodden on; everybody had a right to do what he liked. But inside was the sacred enclosure, cut off from the rest. That was the "fane"; the other was the *pro fanum*. Esau was just that kind of man, not necessarily evil but what we should call secular. God did not enter into his life. There was no sacred enclosure where God reigned supreme. That is why he was spoken of as a "profane person." There are many today of whom this is true. They never fall into gross or open sin. They are not sensual; perhaps only partially are they sensuous. Yet they are living their life altogether separate from God. They are secular; there is nothing devoted to God. Let us therefore keep this thought before us. *Sanctification* in the biblical use of the word is "separateness." There are two words in the Greek, as students know, *hagios* and *hosios*. One means "devoted" and the other means "devout." We are now concerned with the former, and the idea of the Old Testament as well as of the New is a life that is separated from everything that is known to be wrong, a life that is devoted to God at all times.

Sufficiency

"And the house of Jacob shall possess their possessions." Safety, sanctity, sufficiency. There was a vast area of land called originally the holy, the separated land, that Israel had allowed to be taken up by their enemy. God had given it to them, but they had not properly possessed it or kept it. The enemy had taken it; and this promise is that the day would come when they should again enter into their heritage and possess their possessions.

Let us think for a moment of the fact of our spiritual

possessions in Christ—safety and sanctity, with a view to spiritual possessions in Him. Think of those passages that are familiar to us, though they are well worth putting together. "Shall He not with Him also freely give us all things?" (Rom. 8:32). "All are yours" (1 Cor. 3:22). "His divine power has given to us all things that pertain to life and godliness" (2 Pet. 1:3). "Blessed be the God and Father of our Lord Jesus Christ, who has blessed us with every spiritual blessing in the heavenly places in Christ" (Eph. 1:3). So, "accepted in Christ" is intended to mean "endowed in Christ." It is not future, "will bless," but past, "has blessed us with every spiritual blessing." In that wonderful passage, Ephesians 1:3–14, we see that the Apostle, after having stated the fact of all spiritual blessings, proceeds to show how these blessings have come—in the purpose of the Father (verses 3–6); by the purchase of the Son (verses 7–12); and by the power of the Spirit (verses 13–14). Each section of that paragraph ends with a similar phrase. The Father's purpose was intended to be "to the praise of the glory of His grace." The Son's purchase was to be "to the praise of His glory." The Spirit's power was to be "to the praise of His glory." So, whether eternally purposed by the Father, or historically provided in the Son, or personally applied by the Spirit, these are the possessions intended for us, for our abundant provision day by day.

There are many passages in which this specific message is brought before us, but there is one of perhaps special importance. The very heart of the Christian life will be found in Romans 8:1–4, for not only do these verses contain the substance of the gospel for the saint, but there is a wonderful connection between them and the chapters that immediately precede and follow. Verse 1 of Romans 8

POWER

looks back on and takes up Romans 5, "There is *no sort* of condemnation to those who are in Christ Jesus (Greek)." This is how the Christian life begins (Rom. 5:1–11). Verse 2 of Romans 8 takes up chapter 6, "The Spirit of life in Christ Jesus has made me free." The whole of chapter 6 is concerned with freedom. Verse 3 of Romans 8 deals with chapter 7, "What the law could not do"; for Romans 7 is concerned with the powerlessness of the law to give holiness. And verse 4 of Romans 8 is the germ of the rest of that chapter. So we need freedom from condemnation, we need deliverance; we need to realize the powerlessness of the law of holiness, and then the power of the Spirit to enable us to live according to the will of God. This is the sum and substance of spiritual possessions.

Of course, we are also concerned with possessing our possessions, for it is only too possible to have and not to enjoy. There is a familiar story told of a farmer who, after long years of toil, died lamenting that he had so little to leave to his needy sons. The sons had the same idea about their patrimony and thought very little of it by reason of the poverty of the soil and their inability to realize any value in it. So they sold it to men who knew that underneath there was vast mineral wealth, which they turned in due course to good account. The father and the sons were potentially rich, possessors of a wonderful property; yet they did not possess their possessions. The Lord Jesus Christ is to many Christians like a vast estate with infinite possibilities, with wealth unexplored, territory uncultivated, beauties not enjoyed, and produce unused. Yet God is asking each one of us this question: "Are you possessing your possessions?"

Why do Christians so often fail at this vital point? What are some of the reasons God's people do not possess their possessions? One is ignorance. They do not know, they do not realize, what their possessions are in Christ Jesus. Yet God desires us to have illumination, enlightenment, "that we might know the things that have been freely given to us by God" (1 Cor. 2:12).

In other cases it is slothfulness that prevents God's people from entering into their possessions. They have touched the hem of Christ's garment; they have realized something of safety in Him from the penalty of sin, but they do not go forward. There is spiritual sloth, spiritual listlessness, and they do not possess their possessions.

It is self-satisfaction in other cases. They are content with imperfect possession and therefore imperfect enjoyment. They are content with a lower standard of Christian living than God intends them to have. They think we should heed that word: "Be not overly righteous" (Eccl. 7:16). Spiritual self-satisfaction! They believe that we can never accomplish all these things, that we must be content with living for the most part in the experience of Romans 7 and only occasionally getting a glimpse of the glory of Romans 8. Their experience is something like that seen in a most unfortunate hymn, one that should only be sung with vital alterations:

> Fighting, following, keeping, struggling,
> Is He sure to bless?

That is not full Christianity; it comes from the dark ages of the Greek church, one of the hymns that is not completely Christian. We also sing of the guerdon [reward]:

> If I find Him, if I follow,
> What His guerdon here?

POWER

> Many a sorrow, many a labour,
> Many a tear.

But is this all? May we not say:

> If I find Him, if I follow,
> What His guerdon here?
> Many a joy and many a blessing—
> Never a fear!

The latter is not worth much as poetry, but it is truer to the New Testament than the original.

There is another reason we do not possess our possessions, and that is timidity. We are afraid. "Do you know that Ramoth in Gilead is ours, but we hesitate?" (1 Kin. 22:3). That is what many Christians do today; we hesitate. We read about the road to victory. "Who is he who overcomes the world, but he who believes that Jesus is the Son of God?" (1 John 5:5), and "His commandments are not burdensome" (v. 3). The secret of victory is a wholehearted surrender to Jesus Christ as the Son of God. Let us see to it that no timidity keeps us from the Promised Land. It has been pointed out that when the spies came back from the visit to Canaan there were, as someone has said, a majority report and a minority report; very often the minority report is correct. The majority report told them of the wonderful glories of that land but also of the enemies and their own inability. The minority report was equally clear about the glories of the land and about the enemies; but it also said: "We are well able to overcome" (Num. 13:30) because they were thinking not of the Anakim but of God. We must never allow timidity to rob us of any part of our possession in the Promised Land.

GRACE AND POWER

If we look at the rest of Obadiah's prophecy, from verse 18 to the end, we shall find the word *possess* in almost every verse. The one thought running through it is especially that of verse 18, "The house of Jacob shall be a fire," with its assurance of victory. "We are more than conquerors through Him who loved us" (Rom. 8:37). God's purpose for every one of us is enjoyment, the enjoyment of all those things that are ours in Christ Jesus, enjoyment not for ourselves, not for anything in the form of what would be called spiritual luxury, but for service, that we may be able through that enjoyment to pass on the joy and the blessing to others.

What is the secret, the simple, all-embracing secret of this safety, sanctity, and sufficiency? The answer is, faith. Why is faith so emphasized in Scripture? Because it is the only possible response to God's revelation. His faithfulness is to be met by my faith, His truth by my trust. He is trustworthy; therefore I must be trustful. Faith accepts all these things in Christ; faith claims them as our own possession; faith appropriates them to our own personal use; faith uses them to the glory of God.

And this will be the result as we endeavor to possess our possessions. The Christian life is always fourfold. First, it is a life of *inward peace*, the peace of reconciliation, the peace of restfulness—"peace with God" and "the peace of God." Second, it will be a life of *upward progress*, progress in knowledge and progress in fellowship, God's becoming better known and fellowship with God's becoming more fully realized. Third, it will be one of *outward power*, in the sense of victory over sin, power in our equipment for service. Fourth, it will be one of *onward prospect*, the prospect of hope and of its realization. "The blessed hope and glorious appearing of our great God and Savior Jesus

POWER

Christ" (Titus 2:13) will occupy its proper place on the horizon of our Christian life if we are Christians according to the New Testament pattern. A truth that is found so often in the New Testament must have some real meaning, or it would not be so prominent. The Lord's coming is one of the most powerful incentives to holiness. "What manner of persons ought you to be?" (2 Pet. 3:11).

Inward peace, upward progress, outward power, onward prospect—that is Christianity. If only the Holy Spirit enables us to see and to enter into our possessions, we shall live in our homes, go to our work, serve in our church, and continue wherever we may be situated, full of God's blessing, full of His grace, full of His power, to live henceforth as never before to His eternal praise and glory.

XI

PRIVILEGE

The first word of the Psalms, *blessed,* is in some respects the keynote of the whole book. It occurs nearly thirty times. But the interesting point about the beatitudes of the psalter is that they are nearly all concerned with our relation to God; scarcely do circumstances enter into this blessedness. So, according to the Psalms, it is not what we have, or what we know, or what we can do, but what we are, that constitutes blessedness.

One of those numerous passages is found in Psalm 89:15–18, and it shows that the Christian life is a life of privilege in power and blessing. Let us remember, even though it needs constant repetition, we are to know the things that are freely given to us of God; as we look at this passage, we shall be able to see something at least of what the Bible means by the Christian life, that life which we are to meditate upon, to understand and, by the mercy of God, to experience.

A Life of Perpetual Fellowship

"They walk, O Lord, in the light of Your countenance" (Ps. 89:15). The countenance of God is a symbol of the divine presence. The word is literally "face"; and the face of God in Scripture always means His presence. Then it also means the divine favor. "In the light of the king's face is life" (Prov. 16:15). The benediction that was pronounced upon Israel closed with, "The Lord lift up His countenance upon you" (Num. 6:26). It is said of David in relation to Absalom that "the face of the king" was not toward him as before. Thus the idea of the divine face or countenance is His presence and His favor. And, of course, it also implies divine guidance. There is a phrase in the psalm about the servant looking to the master (Ps. 123:2), that is, desiring to know what the master's will is; here we have, "They walk, O Lord, in the light of Your countenance." Walking implies progress, and walking in the light of the divine countenance means guidance as we take our journey and make progress through life.

Walking is one of the illustrations used in the Bible to express spiritual progress. Almost every part of man's body is associated with spiritual things. Sometimes we are to "look" and be saved; at other times we are to "hear" and our souls shall live; at another time we are to "take hold" of God's strength; at another we are to "taste and see." But most frequent of all is the word *walk*. In the brief epistle to the Ephesians it occurs seven times. We recall also the well-known text, 1 John 1:7, "If we walk in the light as He is in the light." So this is the first feature of the new life, a life of perpetual fellowship, in the divine presence, with the divine favor, and under the divine guidance.

At this point it will be well to ask ourselves, What do we know of this? Is this the experience of our life? For this is what the Bible intends. If the Christian life is not a life of perpetual fellowship, it is nothing at all. There are two men who are said to have walked with God, Enoch and

PRIVILEGE

Noah. Many people think Enoch had a very delightful time of it, full of blessed contemplation. But we are told by Jude that he had a very severe experience in testifying against ungodliness; and, therefore, not even Enoch had altogether an easy and quiet life. But whatever we may think about Enoch, Noah was a practical man of affairs. For one hundred twenty years he preached the gospel of righteousness without getting a single convert, though all the while he was walking with God. This is the life intended for us, the life of perpetual fellowship.

A Life of Unchanging Joy

"In Your name they rejoice all day long" (Ps. 89:16). We must not forget, though it is often repeated in our ears, that there is a vast difference between joy and happiness. Happiness depends upon what *happens*, upon circumstance, the "hap" of life. Joy is independent of circumstances and is connected with our relationship to God. Happiness is very much like the surface of the sea, sometimes turbulent, at other times calm; joy is like the bed of the ocean, which is untouched by anything on the surface. Joy, referring to our relationship to God, is threefold. There is the joy of retrospect, as we look back at the past; there is the joy of aspect, as we look around on the present; there is the joy of prospect, as we look forward to the future. There is the joy of memory, the joy of love, and the joy of hope. There is the joy of the peaceful conscience, the joy of the grateful heart, the joy of the teachable mind, the joy of the trustful soul, the joy of the adoring spirit, the joy of the obedient life, and the joy of the glowing hope.

"In Your name they rejoice." That is where we get our

joy—"in Your name," in the revelation of God. The name of God is all that is known of Him. Wherever the word *name* occurs, it never means a mere title or epithet but a character, the revealed character of God. In proportion as we get to know this "name" and what it means in all its fullness, we shall have joy, which will thus depend not upon ourselves but upon God.

"In Your name they rejoice all day long—" in other words, under all circumstances. That is what Paul meant when he said, "Rejoice in the Lord always" (Phil. 4:4). He did not say, "Be happy in the Lord always." He knew very well it was impossible. We cannot be happy always. If we have anything troublesome in our circumstances, if we have any bodily pain, if we have any mental or social anxiety, we cannot possibly be happy. The apostle Paul was not very happy when he called himself sorrowful, but he said, "Sorrowful, yet always rejoicing" (2 Cor. 6:10). While we cannot be happy always, we can rejoice always, because we rejoice in the Lord always. Our joy is independent of happiness, of what happens; it is associated with God.

This, too, is a need of the Christian life, one that ought to be considered again and again, the need of unchanging joy. If in our daily life we do not realize what this means, we are lacking in one of the essential features of biblical Christianity.

A Life of Perfect Righteousness

"And in Your righteousness they are exalted" (Ps. 89:16). What do we mean by righteousness? We might put it in this way and say it means *rightness*, "the state and condition of being right with God." In some respects *righteousness* is one of the greatest words in the Bible. We find it frequently in that large section, Isaiah 40 to 46. But righteousness is also the great message of the apostle Paul. We sometimes think that the essence of the gospel is the mercy of God or the love of God. Paul did not think so. He said, "I am not ashamed of the gospel of Christ... for in it the righteousness of God is revealed" (Rom. 1:16–17). It was because Paul felt that righteousness, even more than mercy, was necessary, that he emphasized it as the keynote of his gospel, the truth of righteousness, the state of being right with God.

The whole of the epistle to the Romans is built up in a sevenfold way on this thought of righteousness: righteousness required, chapters 1 and 2; righteousness revealed, chapter 3; righteousness reckoned, chapter 4; righteousness received, chapter 5; righteousness realized, chapters 6–8; righteousness rejected, chapters 9–11; and righteousness reproduced, chapters 12–16. The entire teaching from the beginning to end is righteousness, which is the meaning of the Christian life—a life of perfect righteousness.

"In Your righteousness." That is the sphere and the atmosphere of true living. "In Your righteousness." It means that we are to be surrounded by that righteousness, covered by it, protected by it. If that is not true of us now, then there will be no blessing until it is settled. Do we know what God's righteousness is? We have no concern with His holiness until we have received His righteousness, for it is only when we possess this that holiness becomes possible. There are those who wish to know the best way of living the holy life. But perhaps they have never made sure of this question of righteousness. This is the primary necessity. "In Your righteousness they are exalted." Exalted above our foes, exalted above our fears, exalted above our failures.

What do we know of God's righteousness? I was taking a walk some years ago with a beloved friend, a well-known clergyman, and as we passed a particular house he pointed to it and said, "I never pass that house without calling to mind this incident. I was summoned to see a lady, an entire stranger to me, and, indeed, to this town, who was thought to be dying. I went in, and I very soon saw that she could not live long. After a few words of personal interest and sympathy, I said to her, 'Now, it may not be God's will that you should recover. May I ask how you regard the future?'" Said my friend, "She opened her eyes wide, and fixed them on me, and said, 'Not having mine own righteousness, which is of the law, but the righteousness which is through faith of Jesus Christ, the righteousness which is of God through faith.'" And my friend added, "That is all she said, and it was quite sufficient." In the same way now, not for death but for life, this is the secret, "Not having my own righteousness, which is from the law, but that which is through faith in Christ, the righteousness which is from God by faith" (Phil. 3:9). This is the thought here. "In Your righteousness they are exalted." And day by day and hour by hour, if this is settled, we are able to sing and able to mean what we say when we sing:

> Jesus, Thy blood and righteousness
> My beauty are, my glorious dress;
> 'Midst flaming worlds in these arrayed,
> With joy shall I lift up my head.

PRIVILEGE

A Life of Complete Protection

"For You are the glory of their strength" (Ps. 89:17). Strength is one of the great needs of the Christian, and it is associated with righteousness. In more than one passage in Isaiah we find both: "In the Lord I have righteousness and strength" (Is. 45:24). Strength follows righteousness here because it refers to the next great need of the Christian life, strength for daily living. There is an old Latin phrase we might almost put into very literal English when we speak of the need of power to "resist," to "insist," and to "persist"—power for everything in the Christian life. The secret of it is, "You are the glory of their strength." Not self, not circumstances, but God is our strength. "You are the glory of their strength." His presence is salvation.

In both the Old and New Testaments the verb *glory* or *boast* is utilized for right and true and pure ideas and ideals. If there is one person who is more contemptible than another, it is a man or woman who boasts. Whenever we find a man boasting, we always feel that he is one of the most deplorable and contemptible specimens of humanity. We know what Uriah Heep means, not only in the pages of Dickens, but everywhere else, the man who is always "very 'umble." Caroline Fry has a fine definition of true humility: "unconscious self-forgetfulness." The self-forgetfulness that is conscious is, of course, the most acute, intense, and subtle form of pride; yet here and in the New Testament this verb *boast* in the original, although often rendered "glory," is taken over and transformed, and we are enabled to boast in a great number of things. "God forbid that I should glory [boast] except in the cross of our Lord Jesus Christ" (Gal. 6:14). We "rejoice [boast] in hope of the glory of God. And not only that, but we also glory [boast] in tribulations" (Rom. 5:2–3). We can glory as much as we like as long as we glory in Him and not in ourselves.

In this connection let us emphasize the word *complete*, because it is intended to mean what it says. At all times, under all circumstances, God's grace is sufficient for us. "Behold, I give you the authority... over all the power of the enemy, and nothing shall by any means hurt you" (Luke 10:19).

A Life of Assured Victory

"And in Your favor our horn is exalted" (Ps. 89:17). The "horn" in the Old Testament is the symbol of conquest, of victory. Wherever the word occurs, it is associated with complete victory. When it says here, "In Your favor our horn is exalted," of course it means that in union and communion with God there is assured victory, as well as complete protection. It may be questioned whether we have ever sounded the depth, or rather scaled the height, of Paul's word, where, in Romans 8:37, he speaks of us as "more than conquerors." One of the French versions is *les vainqueurs et au dela*—"conquerors, and beyond that." Yes, but what is the "beyond that"? It is "superconquerors"; not merely the bare victory, not merely that which just manages to get home, but that which gives us a perfect and abundant conquest over the enemy.

A Christian man, in his humility, said on his deathbed that he would be thankful if he just crept into heaven on his hands and knees. We fully appreciate the spirit in which he said those words; yet God does not expect us or desire us or intend us to creep into heaven on our hands and knees, for has He not spoken of "an entrance [that] will be supplied to you abundantly into the everlasting kingdom" (2 Pet. 1:11)? And this is the thought here, "conquerors and more than that," superconquerors; victory and more than victory assured in the favor of God.

A Life of Absolute Guarantee

"For our shield belongs to the LORD,/And our king to the Holy One of Israel" (Ps. 89:18). Who is our Shield? The Messiah. Who is our King? The Messiah. Who is the Lord? The Holy One of Israel. Therefore it says that Christ, our Messiah, our Shield, our King, belongs to God. That is the meaning of Paul's words, "Christ is God's" (1 Cor 3:23).

This introduces us to one of the profoundest and yet one of the simplest truths of the Bible, the covenant between the Father and the Son on our behalf. If we read very carefully Hebrews 8, we shall see that the new covenant is not between God and us; it is between the Father and the Son. Again and again there is this wonderful thought of a solemn covenant and agreement between God and Christ. We must, of course, use human language to express it, but the idea is of a definite covenant on our behalf. It was this, no doubt, that the psalmist regarded as the culminating point of the believer's life. "Our shield belongs to the LORD,/And our king to the Holy One of Israel." So Paul is not only able to say what I have just quoted but also, "Things present or things to come—all are yours. And you are Christ's, and Christ is God's" (1 Cor. 3:22–23). That also is the meaning of such a passage as John 10:28–29: "I give them eternal life, and they shall never perish; neither shall anyone snatch them out of My hand. My Father, who has given them to Me, is greater than all; and no one is able to snatch them out of My Father's hand." It is well known that philosophy and evolution, and indeed the general trend of modern thought, have during recent years emphasized the human side of things. Perhaps that was the necessary and inevitable rebound from an overemphasis on the divine side some years ago. Be that as it may, we must never forget that there is a divine side as well as a human side. Never let us overlook the fact that God keeps us, and this is prior to our keeping ourselves. An Irish boy was once asked whether he did not sometimes feel afraid. He replied, "I often *trimble* on the rock, but the rock never *trimbles* under me." "I hold," says the motto; but there is another side to it—"and I am held." It is a great thing to hold God by faith; it is a much greater thing for God to hold us with a grasp that never tires. "Fear not, for I am with you;/Be not dismayed, for I am your God./I will strengthen you,/ Yes, I will help you,/I will uphold you with My righteous right hand" (Is. 41:10).

> Let me no more my comfort draw
> From my frail hold of Thee;
> In this alone rejoice with awe,
> Thy mighty grasp of me.

This idea of the covenant has almost entirely fallen out of modern theology and modern writing. We must get back to it as the bedrock of everything. There was a

PRIVILEGE

woman in Scotland on her deathbed, waiting for the end, after forty years of Christian life and service. She was deeply taught of God. Her friends felt they could say pretty much what they liked to her, so one of them remarked, "Well, you have been a Christian forty years; suppose the Lord were to let you go?" "Ah," she said, "He would lose more than I should." She meant that He would lose His character. God has pledged Himself in covenant with Christ on behalf of His people. If you read the great, the *real* Lord's Prayer, not the disciples' prayer that we call the Lord's Prayer, but the Lord's own Prayer in John 17, you will find a reference to the covenant between God and Christ on behalf of those who were given to the Son by the Father, and concerning whom, with one exception, the Lord said, "I have lost none." This is what I mean by the absolute guarantee. It will be worthwhile if we can get down to this basis and realize, apart from all our feelings and circumstances and problems and doubts and needs, the truth of the Lord's statement: "I am the LORD, I do not change" (Mal. 3:6). "The solid foundation of God stands, having this seal: 'The Lord knows those who are His,' and, 'Let everyone who names the name of Christ depart from iniquity'" (2 Tim. 2:19).

A Life of Personal Relationship

"Blessed are the people who know the joyful sound" (Ps. 89:15). The "joyful sound" had reference to two things in the Jewish religion. It was associated, first of all, with the trumpet on the day of Jubilee. Every fifty years the trumpet of Jubilee sounded, and that meant deliverance. And this, translated into the New Testament, means the gospel. "Blessed are the people who know the joyful sound," the sound of deliverance, the note of the gospel. Paul said of the people of Thessalonica, "From you the word of the Lord has sounded forth" (1 Thess. 1:8). They had received it, and they were sounding out that trumpet of Jubilee, of deliverance. Here again we are at the beginning of things. Do we know this? Do we know the "joyful sound" of deliverance? Do we know the Lord Jesus Christ as our Savior? Has He come to us with His Jubilee of deliverance, deliverance from the guilt of sin, deliverance from the penalty of sin, deliverance from the bondage of sin, and deliverance hereafter from the very presence of sin? Deliverance is the great thought of the "joyful sound."

But it means more than this. Trumpets were used oftener than every fifty years; they were employed from time to time to summon people to worship. If we look at the book of Numbers, we find reference to the silver trumpets the priests used on special occasions. According to some authorities, we might render the passage, "Blessed is the people who know the festal shout," in other words, the shout associated with worship. After deliverance comes worship. After the altar outside comes the tabernacle inside, and so the "joyful sound" first means salvation and then worship.

It is for us to face this question, Is this a personal experience? Do we know the "joyful sound"? Do we know what deliverance means? Do we know what worship means? Do we know what it is to have this opportunity of spiritual worship of our Father in heaven? If so, "Blessed are the people."

So we come back to the note with which we started: *blessed.* It has been well pointed out that festivals of gladness are based on religious facts. It is worthwhile remembering that rationalism has never been successful in originating anything glad or joyful. It would be interesting for our missionary brothers and sisters to tell us how many hymnbooks they have found in connection with heathen religions. Heathenism knows nothing about hymnbooks, or joy, or gladness. Joy is the essential of belief, and so we may put it almost in the words of a modern writer, "Where there is faith, there is gladness." "Blessed are the people who know the joyful sound!" The greatest day of joy in the present age is that which is at once a holiday and a holy day, the birthday of Jesus Christ. The angel said, "I bring you good tidings of great joy" (Luke 2:10).

I heard once of a clergyman who looked on the dark side of things. I do not quite wonder at it because he had spent a noble life as a missionary and had got a severe touch of liver. His people used to say that this good man never gave them anything bright or joyful. All his sermons were associated with gloom, until one Christmas Day he announced as his text, "Behold, I bring you good tidings of great joy." The people said, "Now we are going to have a change!" But the main substance of the sermon was a description of the blackness of the time when Jesus Christ was born. That was all he could do! "Blessed is the people who know the festal shout"—that joy which is the keynote of all Christian life.

So let each one ask himself this, Do I know it? Some know it by hearsay; others have read of it in the Bible; but the word *know* in the Old and New Testaments always refers to personal experience. "Blessed are the people who know." Perhaps someone says, "I do not know." Well, there is only one reason we do not, there is only one reason we cannot know. We find it in Psalm 90:8: "You have set our iniquities before You,/Our secret sins in the light of Your countenance." It is because there is some sin between God's face and ours that prevents our knowing the joyful sound. And so we have need to sing and to pray:

> Oh! may no earth-born cloud arise
> To hide Thee from Thy servant's eyes.

If there is any sin unconfessed and unforgiven, this and this only is the explanation why we do not know the "joyful sound." But if we are willing to have that sin removed and blotted out, so that in the King's countenance there will be life and favor, from this time forward we shall know the "joyful sound" and know it increasingly in our experience. It means this, that now and all through life there will be the *test*, there will be the *trust*, and there will be the *taste*. We shall test these things, and God will welcome us in fellowship with Himself. We shall trust Him, and in that trust will come the removal of all the clouds and all the difficulties. And then, all through life there will be the taste. "Oh, taste and see that the Lord is good; blessed is the man who trusts in Him" (Ps. 34:8).

XII

SATISFACTION

The apostle Paul desired that those to whom he wrote might know the things that were freely given to them of God. In his prayers in the epistle to the Ephesians we have, perhaps, the highest revelation of his conception of the Christian life. He prayed in the first of the two prayers that believers might have a spiritual illumination, that the eyes of their heart might be opened to see the wealth of grace stored up for them in Christ and made available for them. The prophet Jeremiah, foretelling something of the great future, was concerned with a similar subject, the possibilities and realities of a divine life in a personal experience. He uttered a magnificent promise and assurance: "My people shall be satisfied with My goodness" (Jer. 31:14). Although, of course, we know that this whole section has its primary and still future interpretation in regard to God's people Israel, there is no reason, as we have already seen, why we may not look at the words in a secondary, spiritual application and think of them as intended for us.

The Christian life surely means this, if it means nothing else, that we may be led to understand as much as possible of those things that are provided for us of God. Many a passage, for example, the outburst of praise from the lips of the apostle Peter (1 Pet. 1), is altogether concerned with those wonderful realities of grace that have been brought near to us in Christ Jesus.

So it will be well to strike this note of encouragement and to give this word of promise to every believer, "My people shall be satisfied with My goodness." We will look at the divine side of the Christian life, at the provision God has made for us, in order that we may realize afresh, and by His grace enter into the life that He desires us to live.

The Divine Splendor

"My goodness." This is God's character; there is nothing higher. "My people shall be satisfied with My goodness" —not greatness but goodness; not glory but goodness; not grandeur but goodness. This goodness of God is seen in nature. The psalmist says, "The goodness of God endures continually" (Ps. 52:1). "The earth is full of the goodness of the LORD" (Ps. 33:5). "You crown the year with Your goodness" (Ps. 65:11). But still more, the goodness of God is seen in revelation: "I will make all My goodness pass before you" (Ex. 33:19). "The LORD God... abounding in goodness" (Ex. 34:6). "We shall be satisfied with the goodness of Your house" (Ps. 65:4). "The goodness of God leads you to repentance" (Rom. 2:4).

This divine character of goodness is intended to be ours, for "the fruit of the Spirit is... goodness" (Gal. 5:22). It is said of Barnabas that "he was a good man" (Acts 11:24). This is in the past tense and reads as though he were dead at the time, but whether or not it is intended as an epitaph, it expresses his character, than which there is nothing finer. "He was a good man." People often discuss their clergy and talk very freely of them. They say, "Yes, when he comes to see me he hasn't much to say, but then, he is such a good man!" "When we go to church he's somewhat dull in the pulpit, but then, he is such a good man!" Well, while we are sorry for all uninteresting people in the pulpit, and also sorry for the man who has not much conversational power in pastoral visitation, yet if it can be said of a clergyman that he is a good man, we may well thank God that it is so, for we have the finest treasure in this world in goodness. We can understand, therefore, the emphasis laid by the New Testament on good works, because good works are the outcome of goodness.

There are two words rendered "good" in the New Testament and applied to works. The one means that which is inwardly and intrinsically good; the other means that which is outwardly beautiful, and for the most part, in the Pastoral Epistles, the phrase translated "good works" might be rendered "beautiful works." There is a similar distinction between the righteous man and the good man in Romans 5. Our works are intended to be at once ethical and beautiful. The two words are often associated with God Himself. God is, of course, essential goodness, but it is helpful sometimes to remember that our Lord said, "I am the good [beautiful] shepherd" (John 10:11), the Shepherd who is outwardly attractive as well as inwardly good.

It is just here where our goodness often fails—it is not beautiful. If our goodness is not at once ethical and beautiful, it fails at a crucial point. There is a story that when someone said of another, "She is the salt of the earth," the reply was, "Salt? Why, she is mustard and pepper and the whole cruet!" Yes, that is the sad meaning of unlovely goodness.

We often emphasize particular virtues to the detriment of other virtues. There are some who emphasize thrift and sacrifice everything to economy. There are others who emphasize generosity and do not pay their debts! There are yet others who emphasize humility and have not an atom of force in their character. There are still others who emphasize individuality and are very much put out if they do not get the chief places in the synagogues. We emphasize one virtue at the expense of another. There are men who pride themselves on their candor, and it degenerates into brutality. One such man once said to John Wesley, "Mr. Wesley, I pride myself on speaking my mind; that is my talent." "Well," said John Wesley, "the Lord wouldn't mind if you buried that!"

We need that characteristic of Christian ethics found only in Christianity, that indefinable something called "Christlikeness." It is the one quality in Christianity that marks off the ethic of the gospel from every other ethic in the world, the combination of strength and sympathy, the blend of tenderness and force, the association of righteousness and love. There is nothing higher than this—beautiful goodness. It is something for us to be able to know; it is something to be able to do; but it is infinitely more *to be*. Wisdom in God is great; power, perhaps, is greater; but goodness is greatest of all. In the definition of the deity in the first Article of the Church of England, He is described as "infinite in wisdom, power, and goodness." And now abide these three—wisdom, power, goodness—but the greatest of these is goodness.

SATISFACTION

THE DIVINE STANDARD

"We shall be satisfied," and the word *satisfied* at once compels us to think. Satisfaction—Is this possible? Is this true? Is this God's will? The ordinary view of the Christian life is for us to have enough but with no thought of absolute and complete satisfaction. The worldling is quite content with his ease; the Pharisee is thankful that he is not as other men; the Stoic is indifferent to all these things; the selfish man pays no regard to others; the conventional believer is quite content with his low standard of morality. The trouble is that we are content with so little.

In one of the Anglican collects for Good Friday we read that our Lord Jesus Christ "was contented to be betrayed." The word has changed its meaning. When nowadays I say, "I am content," I mean that I am barely ready, or I am just ready. I cannot very well avoid it, but I will put up with the difficulty. "I am content." But in the old English the word *content* meant "contained." "He was contained (in other words, He was full of readiness) to be betrayed." The same old English word is found in the Prayer Book Version of Psalm 40:8, "Lo I come to do Thy will: yea, I am content to do it," that is, "I am contained by it." The will of God filled up the whole of our Lord's life, and the Master was "contained" by His desire to do the will of God. That is the meaning here; and the right view of Christian privilege is not merely bread enough, but "bread enough and to spare." As Scripture promises, "I will satiate the soul of the priests" (Jer. 31:14).

Some may not have noticed the figures of speech used in the Bible to express this spiritual satisfaction. Think of the river in this connection, "peace would have been like a river" (Is. 48:18); "drink from the river of Your pleasures" (Ps. 36:8); and "out of his heart will flow rivers of living water" (John 7:38). Remember the symbol in Ezekiel of the waters to the ankles, then to the knees, then to the loins, and then to swim in (Ezek. 47:3–5). Notice Paul's three metaphors, with his nouns and adjectives, *full, abundant, rich*—the fullness, the abundance, and the wealth of God's grace. This is the standard. God can satisfy and God does satisfy our life. He satisfies the past with forgiveness, the present with grace, and the future with glory. He satisfies the past with justification, the present with sanctification, and the future with glorification. He satisfies the past with pardon, the present with power, and the future with peace. So we have, in the familiar phrase, "safety, certainty, and enjoyment." Let us mark it as it appears in the Word of God, especially in the Psalms. Bible students should notice the word *satisfied* as it is found in the psalter. One or two of these will enable us to see the force of what God intends for us here and now. "My soul shall be satisfied as with marrow and fatness" (Ps. 63:5). "Satisfied with the goodness of Thy house" (Ps. 65:4). "With honey from the rock would I have satisfied you" (Ps. 81:16). "In the days of famine they shall be satisfied" (Ps. 37:19). "Who satisfies your mouth with good things" (Ps. 103:5). "With long life will I satisfy him" (Ps. 91:16). No wonder that Isaiah takes up the word and tells us that we shall be satisfied in the time of drought.

Now when Christianity is understood aright, it is intended to lead to soul satisfaction. Let us be very clear and very careful as to what we mean. Are we satisfied? We reply, "Satisfied with what?" Satisfied with our attainments? "God forbid!" Satisfied with knowledge? "Far from it."

SATISFACTION

Satisfied with our experience? "Oh, no." What is really meant, and the Lord is asking it of each one, is, Are you satisfied with Christ? We remember the wonderful word in Psalm 63:1, "My soul thirsts," and then "My soul shall be satisfied" (Ps. 63:5). Are we satisfied with Christ? It is so easy to sing: "Thou, O Christ, art all I want," and then go out and find some part of our satisfaction outside Christ. So here is the truth for the Christian life of every one. It matters not how long we have been Christians. Nor is the question how much we know of our Bible. It is not even a question as to how much we have in heart and mind of orthodoxy, but this one question is supreme: Am I satisfied with Jesus Christ? Is there any part of my life into which He does not enter, intellectual life, social life, recreative life, hopes, ambitions, aspirations, and even physical life? Is there any part of life that finds its satisfaction elsewhere? This is the real test; and this is why we need to ask God's Holy Spirit to convict us of any dissatisfaction, anything in our life that is causing spiritual concern at this moment. It is a sure and certain test that at any time, under all circumstances, we can gauge our own spiritual life by asking this one question, What is Jesus Christ to me now? Am I satisfied with Christ? "My soul shall be satisfied."

The Divine Secret

We look again at this promise: "My people shall be satisfied with My goodness." The divine splendor, "My goodness"; the divine standard, "shall be satisfied"; the divine secret, "My people." Again and again in the Word of God we find a phrase something like this, "I will be their God and they shall be My people." There is no doubt whatever that it is only with a true and full understanding of what "My people" means that we shall find what spiritual satisfaction is in our personal experience.

What then is it? What is it to be the people of God? "My people." It means, first and foremost, pardon. In 1 Peter 2:10 God's people are described as those who had not obtained mercy but now have obtained mercy. If anyone is not certain on this point, all else will count for nothing until and unless we have received God's pardon, for we never can be one of the people of God until we are pardoned. "As many as received Him, to them He gave the right to become children of God" (John 1:12). "You are all sons of God" (Gal. 3:26). How? "By faith in Christ Jesus." It is only too possible for people who do not know this to desire the Christian life in vain. We have to take for granted the fact of forgiveness, the consciousness of pardon, as the first requirement of the Christian life; but if by any possibility there is any reader who does not know this, the way is simple and clear, and "as old as the hills," as we say. It is the way of trust, the way of simple acceptance, and we enter into the number of the people of God as the result of obtaining mercy.

The next mark of the people of God is His possession. In 1 Peter 2:9 they are called "His own special people." They are God's own property, a people particularly His own. First, pardon, then, possession; we belong to God, and He is able to say "My people" if we belong to Him.

The third mark is purity. We are told more than once of those who have to "come out" and to "be separate," and to put away the unclean thing in order that God may be their God and that they may be His people. He is purifying to Himself a people specially His own. Purity is

SATISFACTION

another of the marks of God's people: purity of thought, of motive, of desire, of will, of conscience, and of action.

The last of these marks is praise: "This people I have formed for Myself; they shall declare My praise" (Is. 43:21). Pardon, possession, purity, praise—these are the four infallible marks of the people of God.

Now comes the question, How can all this be ours? It can at once be answered. It is by a threefold way. There must be separation from all known sin; there must be surrender to God; and the outcome of surrender will be service for God. George Eliot once said, "There are many who are living far below their possibilities because they are continually handing over their individualities to others." There are many who are living below their possibilities because they have handed over their individualities to a priest. As long as they do that, they will continue to live below their possibilities. There are others who are living below their possibilities because they have handed over their individualities to a clergyman, and he takes the place of the priest. Although he is only a pastor, they are so dependent upon him that they are living below their possibilities. There are others who are living below their possibilities because they have handed over their individualities to a favorite devotional author. They read and read and read this man's books, imbibing his thoughts and appropriating his ideas for their life; yet all the while they are living below their possibilities. There are others who are liable to live far below their possibilities because they have handed over their individualities to a special speaker or preacher. As long as they do that, they will never realize what God intended them to be and to do.

Let every reader ask himself, Am I handing over my individuality to any man? If this is so—whatever form it may take—then the individuality will never be what it ought to be. Handing it over to someone else will be the destruction of personality and the utter failure to realize its full and proper potential.

But now let us notice this. There are many who are living far below their possibilities because they are *not* continually handing over their individualities to Christ. What we dare not do with man, we must do with Christ. If you and I do not hand over our individualities to Christ, we shall always remain on a lower level of possibility. That is the secret of the gospel. "It is no longer I who live, but Christ lives in me" (Gal. 2:20). This is found in connection with grace. "Not I, but the grace of God which was with me" (1 Cor. 15:10). Whether for life or for service, "no longer I...but Christ," "not I, but the grace of God."

There are two words in the New Testament that go to the very heart of the matter. One word is translated "I hand over," and the other is translated "I commit," "I deposit." If we look at Acts 15:26 we find Paul and Barnabas described as men "who *handed over* their lives on behalf of the name"—not *hazarded*, as the old King James version has it. There is nothing of "hazard" in the original Greek. That is the secret of the power in their lives; they had handed themselves over for the sake of the name. We also find the word in connection with our Lord, who "committed Himself to Him who judges righteously," "deposited Himself with Him who judges righteously" (1 Pet. 2:23). The other word is used of Christians. "Let those who suffer according to the will of God commit their souls [deposit themselves] to Him in doing good, as to a faithful Creator" (1 Pet. 4:19). Well may the apostle Paul say, "I know whom I have believed

SATISFACTION

and am persuaded that He is able to keep [my deposit,] what I have [handed over] committed to Him, until that Day" (2 Tim. 1:12).

This is the New Testament message. You and I, if we would realize our possibilities, must hand over our individualities to Jesus Christ. The words in the Anglican Communion Service must be the language of our lips and of our hearts, "Here we offer and present unto Thee, O Lord, ourselves, our souls and bodies, to be a reasonable, holy and lively sacrifice unto Thee." Then we shall begin to possess our possessions, to be satisfied with God's goodness, and lip and life will say:

Blessed be the God and Father of our Saviour Jesus Christ,
Who hath blessed us with such blessings, all uncounted, all unpriced.
Let our high and holy calling, and our strong salvation be,
Theme of never-ending praises, God of sovereign grace to Thee.

—F. R. Havergal